To Peaches & Jim,
my good friends and
bibliophiles, Fondly,
Gunther

"... tell everybody, tell everything ..."
In a letter from my sister, Betti, 1939

To my much loved sister, Edith,
  who shares these and many more of
    my memories.

Glencoe, Illinois. September 2014

CONTENTS

LIST OF ILLUSTRATIONS i
ACKNOWLEDGEMENTS iii
FORWARD v
FAMILY MEMBERS viii
FAMILY TREE ix
MY STORY 1
    1. My Parents – From Lemberg To Hamburg 1
    2. Gleanings From The Correspondence
       (1913-1923) 8
    3. From Bad To Worse Times 24
    4. Growing Up In Hamburg (1924-1938) 30
    5. Our Deportation From Hamburg
       To Zbaszyn (1938 – 1939) 55
    6. From Zbaszyn To Lwow
       And Otwock (1939) 66
    7. From Otwock To Cardiff (1939 – 1941) 80
    8. From Cardiff To London (1941 – 1946) 104
    9. From London To America (1946-____) ... 123
MAP OF MY JOURNEY 129
EPILOGUE 130
APPENDIX A: More Family Reminiscences 143
APPENDIX B: Translated Correspondence 165

LIST OF ILLUSTRATIONS

1. My Papa 2
2. My Cousin, Leo 5
3. Uncle Harry And Aunt Bessie 8
4. The First Six Zloczower Siblings 14
5. Uncle Nathan's Picture In The Forward
   Of His Book 20
6. My Family With A Group of Celebrants 23
7. My Mother's January 1938 Postcard
   To Uncle Harry 25
8. Simon With Friends 29
9. Me At Three Months 30
10. Benecke Shul 36
11. Hamburg's Main Synagogue 36
12. Talmud Tora Realschule 37
13. My Cousin Margot With Cornucopia 38
14. Me, Age 13 47
15. The Bimah At Benecke Shul 50
16. Our Kindertransport Group Of Boys 79
17. S/S Warszawa 81
18. Photo From My ID Papers 82
19. The Cornes In Cardiff 84
20. My Alien Registration Booklet 87
21. Halewood Shoe Store in Cardiff 93
22. Returned Letters 100-101

23.	Me With the Crummenerls	109
24.	Hampstead Garden Suburb	109
25.	My Ration Book	111
26.	My Center Lathe Drawing	114
27.	Me With The Staff Of Brompton-Fulham	119
28.	H.M.S. Chaser	125
29.	British Warplanes Being Ditched	125-126
30.	Map Of My Journey	129
31.	My Student ID Card	133
32.	At Betty's Wedding	134
33.	At My Wedding	135
34.	Me With Celia, Betty And Ed	137
35.	My Return Visit To Hamburg	139
36.	Sam in Hamburg	143
37.	Sam And I On The Beach At Blankenese	145
38.	Cilli And Her Daughter, Inge	147
39.	Simon At Continental Coffee	149
40.	Julius, Simon, And Me At Simon's Wedding	150
41.	Julius	153
42.	Edith, Age 19, At Tel-Aviv Beach	157
43.	Edith And Her Husband, Shmuel	158
44.	Betti	163
45.	Betti And Me	164

ACKNOWLEDGEMENTS

My children, Elizabeth (Betty) Rice Feder, and Edward H. Rice, have been the prime movers of this project, and it is to them for their help, encouragement and support, that I owe my heartfelt thanks. They have always shown a great curiosity about my past and a commitment to cherish it. My undertaking to preserve and interpret the newly found old correspondence was possible for me only because of my children's investment in it. I am especially indebted to Betty for more than her proofreading. Knowing my story and my thinking, she has helped me refresh my memories and find my voice. Her input has helped me make the book what it is.

Ed has been the computer maven we needed desperately throughout in the course of consolidating the drafts. My profound thanks to him for his lawyerly corrections of my English and for his wise contributions to the editing and proofreading. I also am indebted to him for his patience in formatting and re-formatting the ever-changing manuscript.

Many others, family and friends, have contributed their interest and encouragement in my project. My nephews, Yossi Steinman and Uri Galili, as well as my nieces, Ilana Steinman and Ilana Galili, insisted with typical Israeli chutzpah that nothing less than a published book would do.

Among my friends who knew my story and urged me on, Michael Swarzman, Jim and Marlene Matousek constituted the cheering section to keep me going. In addition to sharing her enthusiasm for my writing, Marcia Danits contributed also her artistry to the design of the cover page, for which I am grateful to her.

My thanks also to Francine Norling for entrusting me with her grandfather's collection of old letters, which preserved a glimmer of my family's life a century ago. This treasure of original family correspondence inspired me to undertake this project. It is to her and to Steven Pollack that I owe thanks for providing the pictures of their grandparents, my Uncle Harry and Aunt Bessie.

FORWARD

Writing my autobiography, at least for the first 21 years of my life, has been an obsession of mine for a long time. Of course, I have told my story to my children and grandchildren, to other members of my family, and even to strangers who were interested in my background. "Where do you come from?" I have heard this question put to me often. People I meet sometimes detect my foreign accent, but cannot identify it, and are curious. After a lifetime in the United States, and having made a great effort to adopt the American argot, I am still recognized as foreign-born by my accent. But I don't mind. In fact, I feel a little flattered at the interest, and am willing to tell my story—at least in outline. But first, in answer to their question, I usually ask, "How far back in my history would you like me to go?" More than just a quip, my answer hints at the several, ever-changing episodes of my early life, as this autobiography tries to recall.

Obsessed with the desire that my past should not be forgotten, I want my story to be also a tribute to my parents to whom I owe my life and my survival, and to my Uncle Harry and Aunt Bessie who brought me to this land where I have spent all my adult years.

Several years ago I felt that my time might be running out. I combed my memory for any recollections I could find, and sat down to write my story. Recalling my past and committing it to paper was a labor of love, but also a cathartic experience. The comforts of home, my ambitions at school, the traumas that followed, the stresses of growing up in England during World War II, and the final journey to America, all came back to me, thankfully with mitigated force. My writing required no research and little editing. I wrote quickly and ended with great feelings of relief. I had fulfilled my task.

Then, a few years ago, I came serendipitously into possession of a collection of letters and postcards addressed to my Uncle Harry in Chicago. The letters are dated from the time he arrived in America in 1913 to the outbreak of World War II in 1939. This mail came from the family he had left behind, in Hamburg, in Bolechow, and in Stryj. (The last two towns are in Galicia.) The collection included letters from my mother, her sister (my Aunt Fanny), and her brother, (my Uncle Nathan). What a wealth of information about their family life in the old times!

As I read my mother's letters to Uncle Harry, I could see her bent over the kitchen table—she was very near-sighted and wore thick glasses—scratching away with pen and ink, pouring her heart out as she wrote. Her sister, Aunt Fanny, who was in her teens and 10 years younger than my mother, had written in a less serious mood. I read her writing with great delight, and was reassured that in her world, not totally shared by the whole family household, there was still some joy. Aunt Fanny seemed to have had the most time and emotional energy to maintain the correspondence from Hamburg where she stayed for a time with my mother. She became the family spokeswoman. Unfortunately, Uncle Harry kept no record of letters he had sent, but from the responding letters I could infer much of what he wrote.

Uncle Harry passed down this precious correspondence to his daughter, Roslyn Pollack, and she passed it on to her daughter, Francine Norling, who in turn entrusted it to me. The letters and postcards were written in German and Yiddish and many were still intact and legible, though the album, in which they had been mounted with bits of Scotch tape, was disintegrating. I carefully removed the letters from the album, then sorted, translated, and preserved them for archival use. The original letters with translations will be stored at the U.S. Holocaust Memorial Museum in Washington, D.C.

Going over, or rather into, this old correspondence, I was impressed by the closeness that all members of Uncle Harry's family showed to one another. In German or Yiddish, along the edges of the paper and into the address portion of the postcards, the writing was filled with love and worry and news about everyone in the family. No spaces were left empty. What emerged between the lines at first, then explicitly, was the urgency and the preciousness of the contact. But there were also appeals to Uncle Harry for help getting affidavits for family members to immigrate to America. Poor Uncle Harry, he often was slow to answer and elicited much scorn and anger as if he had forgotten the family he had left behind. But far from having been insensitive to these appeals, Uncle Harry came through unfailingly for many of them. It was he who provided the papers for my brother, Simon, and later for me, as well as for others of his family, to come to the States. And with that treasure trove of "the old days" now available to me, I felt I had to write yet another, expanded version of my story.

FAMILY MEMBERS

ZLOCZOWER

Parents:
CHAIM ZLOCZOWER   b. 1878, d.1941
LEAH ESTHER, nee Fruchter   b. 1885, d.1941

Children:
Cilli Schieber   b. 1905, d. 2004
Sam Eden   b. 1906, d. 19__(?)
Isaac Zloczower   b. 1910, d. 1929
Moritz Zloczower   b. 1911, d. 1918
Simon Rice   b. 1913, d. 2008
Julius Rice   b. 1914, d. 1996
Edith Galili   b . 1919
Betti Zloczower   b . 1921, d. 1941
Gunther Rice   b . 1924

FRUCHTER
Leah Esther, m. Chaim Z.
Nathan, brother, m.___(?)
Fanny, sister, m. Carlos Kauf

KISTENMACHER
Martin
Cilli, nee Zloczower,
(sister of Chaim Z.)

SCHNEIDER
Munio, cousin (?) of

REISS
Father:
S.A. REISS, b. 18...(?), d.1914*

Children:
Morris Rice
Max Rice
Dora Nechamkin
Herman ("Harry") Rice, m. Bessie Itzkovitz;
    Rosalyn, daughter of Harry R., m. Sam Pollack;
        Steve Pollack, grandson of Harry R.
        Francine Norling, granddaughter of Harry R.

---

*After his first wife passed away, S.A. Reiss (Harry Rice's father), married my maternal grandmother, who was a widow. Each brought children to this marriage. This is how my mother's family combined with the Reiss family.

FAMILY TREE

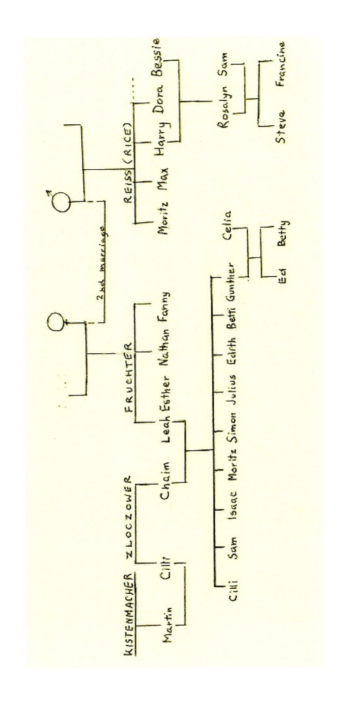

MY STORY

1. My Parents – From Lemberg To Hamburg

I was born into a Polish-Jewish family in Hamburg, Germany, on 20 October 1924, but my story does not begin with my birth. Nor does it start with my earliest memory. It begins with what I remember about my parents' background and what I later learned about their life starting from the turn of the 20th Century. Not that they ever talked about their parents or their childhood. What little I know comes also from my brothers and sisters, who were not exactly fountains of information. The life that our family led did not allow for any story telling. In retrospect, I think we were all in "survival mode." For my parents to recall their past was, at best, an indulgence or irrelevance and, at worst, a dangerous diversion. Through exploring my family's postcards and letters to my Uncle Harry, however, I have been able to draw a better picture of my parents' life between the two World Wars.

My father, Chaim Zloczower, was born on 18 October 1878 in Lemberg (later known as Lwow in Polish, and now Lviv in Ukraine). While his name no doubt originated with people who came from the town of Zloczow, also located in Galicia (near Lemberg), we have never known any ancestors from that town. Lemberg was a large city in the province of Galicia. It once was part of the Austro-Hungarian Empire and, at one point, had been its capital. At the end of the 19th Century over 31,000, or 21% of its total population, was Jewish,[†] but its impact on East European Jewry was even greater than these numbers suggest. Lemberg was a hub of Jewish cultural and political activity. Chasidim and Maskilim, two competing religious movements, and Zionists, struggled for control and power in the Jewish community, but I don't think my parents were politically active. My parents both came from working class, religiously observant homes.

I imagine the environment in which my dad grew up was probably not unlike the self-contained Jewish neighborhood in Hamburg where I grew up. Though he lived in the center of Chasidim, my father was not one of them. He didn't go to a *cheder*. His education at the German-Jewish schools that were functioning then in Galicia included secular as well as Jewish subjects. Nonetheless I looked up to him as being well steeped in Jewish tradition. With the defeat of the Austro-Hungarian Empire and the restoration of Galicia to Poland in 1919, my parents' nationality became officially Polish, although they were already living in neighboring

My Papa
Hamburg, 1915

[†] YIVO Encyclopedia of Jews in Eastern Europe: "L'viv." (http://www.yivoencyclopedia.org/article.aspx/Lviv)

Germany. That political procedure, unpredictably, proved to be fateful 20 years later.

My mother was born in Bolechow (now Bolekhiv, in Ukraine) on 20 November 1885, and her name was Leah Esther Fruchter.‡ Bolechow was one of the small towns in the area, some 75 miles south of Lwow, with a population of 4,402 in 1890 of whom half were Jewish.§ Tradesmen, rabbis, and visitors of all sorts would come to Bolechow from Lemberg and its surrounding areas, particularly on weekends or market days. Our family legend has it that my debonair father on his trips to Bolechow charmed my mother with his good looks and with his singing. He wooed her with his voice and spirits. (Much later those spirits were mostly *bronfen*, but he never drank to excess.) He used to sing liturgical songs with his sweet tenor voice, perhaps having inherited it from his father or grandfather who was said to have been a rabbi or *chasan* (cantor), though this was never confirmed. On a Friday night people in Bolechow would gather around my mother's house by the open window to hear him and to join in the singing.

The earliest picture I have of my dad is from 1915 when he was 37 years old. It was taken in a Hamburg studio during the second year of World

---

‡ The correspondence never mentions my maternal grandmother. I can only speculate that she may have died before 1908, when my parents left for Hamburg, or possibly about four years earlier when my parents got married and lived in Lemberg.

§ www.jewishencyclopedia.com/articles/3482-bolechow.

War I. At the time he was the father of 6 children and working as a turner, making round wooden objects, like table legs or chess pieces, on a lathe. In the picture he looks like a German "burgher" with a small mustache adorning his Slavic face. His eyes look out from under his brows with gentleness and uncertainty. But I knew him only in his later years as a "chevraman," a very social man, who knew how to enjoy himself given the opportunity. I remember him as someone who loved to hang around with friends and acquaintances in the Jewish community or, when home, indulge himself with some rest on the sofa and a cigar. He was usually in good humor and, judging from what I gleaned from my mother's mournful reproaches, he had an eye for women.

I knew my mother only as a serious, introverted type, and inclined to be depressed, in contrast to my extroverted, easygoing father whose liveliness must have appealed to her. That appeal may have faded when baby after baby arrived. She took the burdens life imposed on her like a martyr. She had a very strong conscience and believed in God, which saw her through the tough times.

My parents were married in Galicia by a rabbi, never in any civil ceremony, at least not until later in Germany. They then realized they had better get a German marriage certificate to make their children legitimate. My father was 25 years old and my mother was 18 when they married in 1904. Their first child, my eldest sister Cilli, was born a year later (1905), followed by my brother Sam, the next year (1906). When Cilli's son-in-law, Oded, visited Hamburg many decades after the World War II, he searched the city archives and made a surprising discovery: my parents' marriage certificate. Not only did this provide rare documentation of their very existence, it also revealed the first names of my father's parents: Schmuel and Tsivye. I was surprised and amazed. Evidently my father had named his first-born children, Sam and Cilli, after his parents. Since we name our children in the Ashkenazi tradition only after *deceased* members of the family, it is clear that my father's parents were no longer alive when his first children were born.

Of my father's siblings I know only his younger sister, Cilli, who also left her home town, Lemberg, to settle in Hamburg, probably before W.W.I. She married a Jewish egg merchant, aptly named Kistenmacher (crate maker). They lived in our neighborhood and we often got together with their children; Leo, a few years older than I, but closer to my brother Simon, and Margot, about my age.

My Cousin, Leo

They immigrated to Argentina in 1938 with their children and a brand-new baby, Jacob. About 70 years later Margot's granddaughter, Eliana Vincente, contacted me from Buenos-Aires. She was a relative I did not know, and a voice I had never heard. She handed the phone to her anxious grandmother, Margot, who was already quite ill and wanted one last opportunity to talk again with me. It felt almost unreal. For those brief moments it wasn't the poorly understood words we exchanged that bridged the many decades of silence, it was the realization that we both had survived.

I also had an Uncle Munio, on my father's side, but I never heard much about him when I grew up. Although I got to meet him and his family in 1939 when my parents, Betti and I landed in Lwow, I could not find his place on my father's family tree. I did get to know him, however, from his letters and from what Betti wrote to me about him.

My mother brought to her own young family a personal history that shaped the direction of all her years that were to come. She must have been a teenager when her father died, and her mother's mourning left her in charge of her orphaned younger siblings, Nathan and Fanny. In this small town, Bolechow, lived also a widower with several children who needed a mother for his brood. His name was S. A. Reiss. As was the custom in the Jewish community, he married my maternal grandmother, forming a reconstituted family. Like a tree that has been pruned, giving it fresh life, the new union became the foundation of a strong, very close family, to which the correspondence I have obtained amply attests. My Uncle Harry's father, S. A. Reiss, was most beloved by the whole family, judging by the outpouring of concern and compassion when he fell ill and when he passed away. Although there were now many stepsiblings, not one letter addressed or referred to a *step*brother or *step*sister—they were only brothers and sisters. And the reciprocated love and concern for every one of them was unmitigated. (It was only when the postal service failed and the absence of mail caused great anxiety, that fear, frustration, and even angry accusations were voiced in the letters.)

I could not find out whether my parents in the first year or two of their marriage lived in Lemberg or Bolechow. If tradition is a reliable guide, it was probably Lemberg, my father's hometown. It was not later than 1907 when my dad made the decision to take his wife and two babies to America. A virtual mass migration of East European Jews to *"The Goldene Medineh" (The Golden Country)* was already underway, and my dad set off by himself, joining those many young men who were making the long journey without their families in the hope of bringing them over to America as soon as they could afford it. The route led overland to Hamburg, Germany's major port on the North Sea, where ships were plying regularly the Atlantic route to New York.

My dad probably had brought with him only enough money to pay for a ticket on the steamer, because he soon ran out of cash and turned to the local Jewish community for help. Outgoing and enterprising as he was, he felt comfortable in their midst, found work, and was easily persuaded to stay. Why then risk a sea voyage and go to a strange land? He knew and spoke Yiddish, German and Polish fluently, and was for a time an interpreter in Hamburg. The Jewish community welcomed him. He felt he had found his niche, and he saw a future for himself and his family. With the arrival of my mother and her two little babies, Cilli age 2 and Sam 1, a year after he had settled, ca.1908, Hamburg became their new hometown, and their new home became the way station for the Reiss contingent on their way to America.

2. Gleanings From The Correspondence (1913-1923)

My Uncle Harry was not the first of the Reiss clan to make the long trip to America from Bolechow by way of Hamburg. His brothers, Morris and Max preceded him. But we were closest to Uncle Harry, who saved the correspondence that recorded so much family history. In the winter of 1913, eleven years before I was born, Uncle Harry stayed with my parents for a short time in Hamburg before he embarked on his new life across the Atlantic. He was 18 years old. He had lost his mother many years earlier and, when the two families merged, my mother, who was 10 years older, became his big sister. My mother remembered how they played as children, adding in a letter to him that the mere memory of it made her feel young again. My mother remained close to Uncle Harry, and throughout the years that followed, right up to the Nazi invasion of the Soviet Union in 1941. Uncle Harry made great efforts to provide immigration papers not only for members of his family, but also for my brother Simon and later for me. Obtaining

Harry & Bessie Rice

immigration papers for European relatives at that time was no easy task. When my Uncle Harry managed to get the necessary affidavit for Simon, my mother was overcome with gratitude that her son was rescued. (Uncle Harry did the same for me after the war, though my parents were no longer alive to celebrate this fulfillment of their dream.)

Five years after arriving in America (and settling in Chicago) Uncle Harry fell in love with a woman, Bessie Itzkovitz, who converted him from a "greenhorn" into a respectable American. (When I came to this country in May 1946, Aunt Bessie quickly transformed me, too—at least in dress and appearance.) Uncle Harry and Aunt Bessie married in Chicago in 1918. My Aunt Bessie was a warm, intelligent, can-do (and will-do) woman. Her parents were Jewish immigrants from Eastern Europe. She had one brother, two sisters and many nephews, nieces and cousins in this country. And everyone acknowledged her as the head of the entire extended family.

In Bolechow, Uncle Harry trained as a tailor, but I do not know what vocation he pursued during his first five years in America. But shortly after he married Aunt Bessie, the two went into business. They opened a clothing store for women, children and infants, and they lived above the store on Fullerton Avenue on Chicago's West Side. Even with all the pressures of making a living, adjusting to the American culture, and meeting his family responsibilities, Uncle Harry maintained his close contact with the family he had left behind. Soon after his arrival in America he must have reached out to his family conveying the hardships he felt. He did not have to wait long for an answer.

"My Dear Brother Herman," Aunt Fanny wrote in her letter to him on 9 March 1913, (1) "I have not heard from you for such a long time ... I want to let you know that the letter you had sent to Laura [my mother, Leah Esther] arrived already long ago ... we got quite concerned that you had to torment yourself ... for the bad times you have had." Troubled and homesick, Uncle Harry had apparently turned to his sister, my mother. I wish I had that earlier correspondence and could have seen my mother's response to her younger brother. Undoubtedly, she must have been empathic and helpful. Decades later he told me how much he had loved her.

By the time she wrote this letter to Uncle Harry, Aunt Fanny was in Hamburg, having followed my mother there from Bolechow. Not quite out of her teens, Fanny was a spirited girl, with a love of life. Unburdened by the stress of the times, she proved to be the best correspondent and became the spokeswoman for the entire Hamburg family. In her letters she reported all the family news: who got engaged, who got married, who was ill, who was drafted, who went to Siberia, and who was a war casualty. To my great surprise I found out from her letters to Uncle Harry that my dad had to report for induction into the German army in 1915, which must have given him quite an unnecessary scare. After all, he had a Polish passport and therefore could not be drafted. He needn't have worried. At that time, his Polish nationality stood him in good stead.

By the outbreak of World War I in July 1914, my mother was becoming increasingly busy with her burgeoning household. She now had six children, the youngest being Julius, only 7 months old. My father was no longer a turner; he had become the owner of a second hand furniture store and was now a proud businessman. His life mostly involved other members of the Jewish community and he probably spent more of his free time with them than with his own family. Early on, Germany did not feel the war's costs and it did not seem to affect my family directly. My mother complained in her letters only about prices rising, but since she had been used to living a spartan life, or perhaps because she felt it would be a sin for her to complain (after all, there were many people much worse off than she, which I heard her say many times) she characteristically mitigated her complaints in the same letter, often stating that, in spite of the ever growing price increases, "we are not in any need whatsoever." Even as life in Europe grew more and more difficult, my mother never asked Uncle Harry, who by now had a successful business in Chicago, to send money or help with any material needs.

To my surprise my mother never mentioned in all her correspondence any discrimination or violence against Jews in Hamburg during the war years (1914-1918). While news reports from that time suggest that anti-Semitism had become prevalent throughout Germany, it still had not yet hit home. I know that my parents read the war news in the newspapers. Yet they would not write about that. The precious space in their letters and postcards was reserved for more personal information.

Like Uncle Harry, Uncle Nathan traveled from Bolechow to Hamburg on his way to America, and looked to Uncle Harry for help in obtaining an immigration affidavit. Judging by a postcard he sent to Uncle Harry on 6 February 1914, (2) Uncle Harry had promised to get him the documents, but had not been able to deliver them that quickly. Uncle Nathan, impatient to leave Germany before war broke out, was frustrated by the delay. His tone in the card was indignant, though he said nothing to Uncle Harry about the reasons for his urgency. Unable to wait any longer for the affidavit, Uncle Nathan found another way out of Germany—just weeks before Germany went to war.

On 10 May 1914 (3) he wrote to Uncle Harry that he had arrived in Buenos Aires. Unlike most other countries that would let Jews in only on limited quotas, Argentina opened its doors to Jewish immigrants. Uncle Nathan didn't know what to expect in this new country, which he found impoverished and primitive. As I learned from later correspondence, he at first felt miserable and ready to return to Hamburg. But he persevered, married, had children, and embarked upon a successful journalism career. Yet in his initial postcard from Buenos Aires Uncle Nathan did not belabor his struggle in adjusting to his new country. He expressed only his concern and feelings for Uncle Harry's father. "I felt very bad when Leah Esther wrote me that he was very ill, but I'm very glad that your dear father finds himself now, thank God, in good health."

On 30 June 1914 (4) a postcard arrived in Chicago from Aunt Fanny in Hamburg. She wrote she had received the sad news that Uncle Harry's father was very ill. "I don't believe you can imagine how this affects me. Only God in heaven knows … it is sad enough that we first hear of father's illness from Chicago." She chided the family in Bolechow for not having first sent her the news. Unaware of the difficulty in getting mail out of Galicia after the war broke out, she assumed that her family was neglecting to keep in touch with her.

My mother began to write more often after her postcard of 1 December 1914 (5). The war in Europe was now in its 4th month, but daily life for the most part went on as usual. My mother noted in her postcard that she had received only one letter of three that Uncle Harry claimed to have sent her. She referred to the war only in passing, expressing her hope that it would end in victory for her adopted country. She wrote: "regarding the war, you can read everything in the papers …. May God protect and help everyone and lead Austria and Germany to victory."

As I read this correspondence, many years later, I was disturbed that my parents had sided with Germany. On the other hand, I understood why they felt loyal to their new home country. Their daily life, no doubt, was better in Hamburg than it had been in Galicia. Nonetheless, their move to Germany still did not provide them with any sense of security. My mother's "we're okay" sentiment surely overstated the family situation at the time, and she abandoned that tone as the war progressed.

She conceded that running the household was getting costly, but she would not give in to any fear about holding out financially. She wrote, "many items are a little more expensive, so you have to make do," and went on to say in her Yiddish-inflected German, "we don't know anything here, in Hamburg, from need." She went on to say that "Chaim [my dad] is so far still working." That reassurance, however, did not sound hopeful and, indeed, it was short-lived. Yet in her writing about

The First Six Zloczower Siblings
(Right to Left) Cilli, Sam, Isak, Moritz, Simon, Julius

Uncle Harry's father in Bolechow, she sounded more worried, more so than about her own situation.

Seven months later, Aunt Fanny's postcard of 23 January 1915, (6) reveals more about the war's effect upon the family. She wrote, "Groceries are significantly more expensive..." and added rather incongruously, "the weather isn't pleasant either." She also chastised Uncle Harry for sending war news from the U.S., and seemed defensive: "What you had told her [my mother] about the war, we know here, too. Germany publishes the whole truth in all newspapers ... we also get [Yiddish] newspapers from Buenos Aires ...." But in the same card, Fanny informed Uncle Harry about "a minor matter": "Laura [my mother] gave birth to a boy on January 2, with the name Julius. He is the fifth boy. What do you say to that?"

Aunt Fanny was still living with the family in Hamburg, Rentzelstrasse 104, when she wrote in a letter, dated 12 March 1915 (7) that they had taken in two Russian Jews, presumably refugees. I don't know whether they contributed to the rent or whether my mother took them in purely as a *mitzvah*. Aunt Fanny, who had just celebrated her 20th birthday on the first of the month, apparently made a great impression on the new boarders. She wrote, "they made me a present of a very big album of picture postcards," adding unabashedly, "If it is not too much trouble for you, send me some time a beautiful card. Am I perhaps too impudent?" Following her aunt's example, my sister Cilli, who was about 10 years old at the time, also meant to lay claim to Uncle Harry's attention. So she added a couple of lines to the card. After all, her American uncle was an important, much talked about person at home. She addressed her note "Dearest Friend Hermann" and finished her few words with "Your little girl friend, Cilli."

Aunt Fanny heard from Uncle Harry that his father had died and she responded immediately in her letter of 24 November 1915 (8). "Believe me, Hermann, I cried no less than you. When I'm alone and think about it my heart bleeds, and I can't believe that I will never see my father and Yossele again." Apparently Yossele was another family member, but I am not clear about him or his fate. Dora, Uncle Harry's younger sister, was presumably now the last family member remaining in Bolechow, so Aunt Fanny took it upon herself to get Dora out. "I will make sure that she will, first of all, learn to write and speak German, and then learn some trade ... I will go this Sunday to the main railroad station and find out how one travels nowadays [from Bolechow to Hamburg] .... Should she lack the fare I will take care of it."

That same letter (8) held a hint of an old family secret. "Please tell Morris," Aunt Fanny wrote, "to keep absolutely secret what I have told him about Cilli Zloczower." This enigmatic note probably refers to the fact that little Cilli had lost an eye in an accident sometime earlier. Family legend has it that my father somehow, unintentionally, was responsible for the accident, which became a closely kept secret. Cilli was always very self-conscious about her prosthetic eye, although it was not particularly noticeable.

It was now a year and a half into the war and my mother's writing, dated 25 January 1916, (9) reveals her stoic optimism. Uncle Harry probably had expressed his concern about the family he had left behind, but this time my mother showed a little *sang-froid*. "All of us are so far alright... For sure, [the situation 'back home' in Bolechow] is sad, but whoever is alive hopes to live to see better times." She was clearly less worried about herself than those who were suffering. "The people caught up in this present evil war are to be pitied. May God soon send them peace."

Despite the dark times, my Aunt Fanny managed to convey some lightheartedness in her correspondence. In a postcard to Uncle Harry, dated 26 February 1916 (10), she writes, " Since you have invited me to your birthday, I will invite you to mine ... I will be 21 on ... [?] Adar, according to the Jewish calendar, I can hardly believe it myself." Aunt Fanny, always fond of her brother, seemed to address him with some pleasure at being newly grown-up.

The "Great War To End All Wars" ended on 11 November 1918, but I found no family correspondence in my collection for the 9 months period following the war to reveal how the family fared during that time. Perhaps these letters were lost or discarded. Germany's defeat must have shocked my mother, who had hoped for the peace and normal life that she expected to follow Germany's victory. Instead, Germany was defeated and became a breeding ground for the catastrophic rise of the Nazis. The correspondence that followed now began to reflect the family's growing anxiety, eventually to the point of desperation.

Aunt Fanny's letter of 17 August 1919 (11) bridged the communication gap. She was mostly concerned, and confused, about the postal service. "It said in the paper that mail from America will soon arrive, but I came up empty. And so I enjoyed in my imagination getting a sign of life from you. Unfortunately I didn't [get a letter]... in May 1917 I sent you as well as Morris [Uncle Harry's brother] a letter which was returned to me." Evidently unaware that mail from Chicago to Hamburg stopped after America entered the war, Aunt Fanny chided Uncle Harry for having forgotten his sister ... "or what else shall we think of it?" Under such stressful conditions, lack of news or of some response easily gives rise to doubt and suspicion.

In other family news, Aunt Fanny wrote that her brother, Nathan, was very unhappy in Buenos Aires, and thinking of leaving Argentina. (He didn't.) Like a blossoming young girl, Aunt Fanny could now put aside her wearisome thoughts and be a little flirtatious. "How do you like it, Herman, how prettily I make myself up?" She probably had enclosed a picture of herself in a previous letter, and had thanked him for his picture, which he had sent her in turn. She tried to entice Uncle Herman and Uncle Morris (asking "if he is still unmarried") to come to Hamburg "on a pleasure trip, since the military is no longer in power, and you can come freely without any punishment. That would be marvelous!"

The Treaty of Versailles that ended World War I brought in its wake the Great Depression in Germany. And it was devastating to the Zloczower household. My father, who had become a storeowner and had pinned his hopes on growing his business, lost his second-hand furniture store and his dream. To make ends meet, he used his skills to make small deals. He became a traveling salesman. He traveled to South Germany, which had a large Catholic population, selling religious pictures and artifacts. Like Willy Lohman in Arthur Miller's play, Death of a Salesman, my Papa was a beaten man, unable to hold his head up high. He had to rely on his oldest children, Cilli and Sam, to help with the finances.

The first death in the Zloczower family occurred in 1918 when 7-year-old Moritz died as a result of a raging infection. I have a vague memory of what I must have heard: my mother desperately applied cold compresses to little Moritz, which did not bring his fever down. When he died, my mother blamed the doctor for having given her wrong instructions. I could not find any word of this tragic event in the correspondence. As if to compensate for her loss, my mother gave birth to another child the following year. After having borne 5 boys in a row and losing one, my mother finally had the girl she wanted. Edith was born on the 10th of January 1919. Did my mother find any consolation when she nursed little Edith? Could her joy have displaced her mourning? I will never know.

In a long letter, dated 28 October 1919, (12) Aunt Fanny wrote: "Here in Germany everything looks pretty bad … the cost of everything is sky high…our currency has no value abroad … many people here get packages from America with groceries as well as clothing and laundry items … the terrible war and the appalling peace wrecked the best years of our youth …." She did not hesitate to describe honestly how bad things were. She may have been preparing for the appeals that were to come. But there was also "cheerful news" as she put it. Aaron Waldman, a distant relative or friend who had disappeared, turned out to have been imprisoned in Siberia for the past 6 months. Though life in Siberian gulags was nothing to cheer about, the good news was that he was alive. "We have sent him 10 Marks so that he has something for himself." How remarkable and very generous of her in spite of the fact that "the times are very bad. The exchange rate rises from day to day." Also things were going badly for Uncle Nathan in Argentina, but Aunt Fanny wrote: "I cannot help him." For once, it seems, my aunt's compassion outran her resources.

One month later, on 22 August 1922, (13) Aunt Fanny's brother, Nathan, took his turn to write. And he did so in Yiddish on company stationery. No longer the depressed immigrant homesick for Europe, Uncle Nathan had found a job, working as a correspondent for "Die Presse," a Yiddish newspaper publisher. Though he was not making much money, he thanked God that he was now doing better. Many years later when the National Yiddish Book Center in Amherst, MA, reported that it had salvaged a large number of Yiddish books from Buenos-Aires, I inquired whether it had any of Uncle Nathan's publications. They did; not only his 2-volume history of Argentina, but also two other books—all written in Yiddish. (I have them now in my collection.)

Uncle Nathan's Picture In The Forward Of His Book

The next letter from Aunt Fanny is dated 25 September 1922 (14). From her addresses it appears that she had moved twice: once, to another apartment near my parents in Hamburg, and then to

Amsterdam, probably en route to Argentina. In her letter she wrote that she was happy to announce her unofficial engagement to an egg merchant. "Now hear this, dear brother Herrman. I returned [to Amsterdam] from Hamburg last week. I went there for a visit to Chaim [my father] for 14 days and met an acquaintance, a young man who asked for my hand, which I gladly granted him. Although I have known him already a couple of years, we had been like strangers to each other. And now that I have been with him, we got engaged, not officially, but on our word. He is 37 years old and very, very industrious, good, and most of all has a good character… I am very satisfied with my choice and hope we will be suited to each other." Aunt Fanny was 27 at the time. We had no arranged marriages in our family, but Aunt Fanny seemed to adhere to our traditional values: her future husband had to have good character and be able to support a family. Aunt Fanny did not marry this man, however. After she immigrated to Buenos Aires, she married Carlos Kauf, a Jewish merchant from the old country.

Aunt Fanny also had other news: my mother and older sister did not seem well. "Leah Esther, I'm sorry to say, looks very bad, also her oldest daughter, Cilli. She probably studies too hard. On 1 October she will start her job in an office. To her credit, Leah Esther has some very fine children." I was not surprised to read that my mother had looked ill; I remember my mother as a worn-out martyr. She cared for everyone in the family except herself. By this time there were seven children in the family, including Betti who was born on 4 November 1921. Cilli again was called upon to help with the care of yet another baby. And Betti was not the last in line. That precious position fell to me some three years later.

My effort to construct the family history was frustrated by a 10-year gap in Uncle Harry's collection of letters, which contains no mail between 1922 and 1932. However, there appears to have been some exchange of letters during this time. In fact, in the next letter, dated <u>26 July 1932</u> (15) that Aunt Fanny wrote from Buenos-Aires, she reminded Uncle Harry that she had written to him earlier, but had not received a reply. She wrote, "you are [now] answering it … you know already from my last letter that I got married 3 years ago … exactly on our anniversary we celebrated the *Bris* of our son." And she mentioned that she was pregnant again, and also that "Nathan has 2 children: one daughter of 9, and a son, age 2." The family tree was blossoming.

Although family news during the 10-year hiatus was so very limited, I found it enlightening to research the economic conditions at that time on both sides of the Atlantic as a background to our family's life. The 1920's in Germany were politically and economically tumultuous times. Germany's Weimar Republic was short lived; it collapsed as Nazism was on the rise. And the hyperinflation reached astronomical heights. (In July 1924 the exchange rate was 1.2 sextillion Marks to one dollar.) The Wall Street crash in the U. S. came at the end of that decade. I tend to think that everyday life during that time in Chicago, where Uncle Harry lived, no less than in Hamburg, was fraught with existential worries.

I have often looked back and wondered how the turbulent and deadly events in Germany in the 1920s affected our family. My mother certainly must have been aware of the growing threats to the Jews, both physical and economic. She knew there was no future for any of us in Germany, and she was preoccupied with getting her children to safety, though I did not know it at the time. In the 1930s, my brothers and sisters left home, one-by-one. When they left, did my mother wonder she would ever see Cilli, Sam, Simon, Julius, and Edith again? I hold in painful awe her courage in sending away all her children (Betti and I were still too young) knowing only that she gave them a chance at life. She was not thinking of herself; two more children needed to be rescued. Her decision was her ultimate sacrifice.

My Family With a Group of Celebrants Hamburg (undated)

Front Row (far left: my parents and Rosie Glattner; far right: Sam); Second Row (far right, Julius); Third Row (far right, Simon; fourth from right, Cilli; sixth from right: Heini Glattner)

3. From Bad to Worse Times

The year 1938 was the most soul-wrenching time of my life. Events cascaded and so did the overseas correspondence. This was a critical year for all Jews in Germany. The practice of Jewish doctors and lawyers was restricted to Jewish clients. Jewish businesses and community organizations were severely curtailed. A Nazi decree authorized the seizure of Jewish assets. The Polish government threatened in March to revoke the citizenship of Polish Jews living abroad, and made good on its threat six months later.

My mother who saw the handwriting on the wall began pleading more plaintively for Uncle Harry to help Simon immigrate to America. In a postcard, dated 10 January 1938, (16) my mother bitterly complained (again) to Uncle Harry that he had not responded to any of her earlier letters. Time was running out. She could not have known how much time it would take to prepare the papers and for the affidavit applications to grind their way through the bureaucracy. With Cilli, Julius, and Edith already safely out of Germany, my mother pushed for Simon to find safety in America. Unlike her earlier correspondence, in which she wrote in German, my mother wrote this postcard in Yiddish. I have no doubt that this was her attempt to appeal to Uncle Harry more intimately.

In her next letter, dated 9 March 1938, (17) written in German longhand, she poured out her feelings and her fears.

My Mother's January 1938 Postcard To Uncle Harry

I have received your letter and thank you from my heart … although you did not write, I had faith in you … well, I was not disappointed … first I wanted you to know that Simon's biggest wish is to immigrate to America. He is 25 years old and has the best upbringing

... you will never regret it if you would arrange immigration papers for him. He has a good character and knows several languages. To remain in Germany is impossible, and it is my greatest wish to know that the children are in a safe place. That you will understand ... that is our biggest worry: to get the children out of here. Who knows what will happen, he may not be able to get out any more. I want to say again: it will not cost you a cent, and you will have much joy from him because he is cultured and will make a living for himself.

Upon reading my mother's correspondence, I was very moved by her urgent effort to see Simon already safely in America. To my surprise, however, my mother had also attempted the Argentina option for him. "My sister [-in-law, Cilli], Fanny, and Nathan are in Buenos Aires, and they went to some trouble to make it happen [get the immigration papers], but nothing became of it. If he [Simon] were a farmer it might be possible for him to get the immigration papers [to Buenos Aires]. And illegally he would never go."

Having tried to reassure Uncle Harry of Simon's good qualities, my mother also needed to vent her long held angry suspicion of the effect of American culture and way of life on Jewish immigrants, fearing that Uncle Harry, too, may have succumbed to that process of acculturation that curtails feelings of nostalgia. "I fail to understand how business can top all humanity. Ours is not a small town, everyone is busy with his occupation. Yet no one forgets his fellow man. America seems to take away all idealism." There was more worrisome news about Cilli and her husband, Sally (pronounced Zally), about their indigence and Cilli's poor health, but she was reluctant to elaborate further. "I do not want to write more, because it is nothing good."

In this long letter of March 1938, my mother updated Uncle Harry about the rest of the family

> I have a son [Julius] in Palestine, who learned well the furrier trade. He also goes to sea. He is 23 years old, and married. His ship goes to Haifa and Constanta (Romania), and he gets 4 Pounds monthly with which he furnishes his home little by little. Till now his wife also has a job. I still have a daughter [Edith] who was 19 in January and will graduate from the WIZO school in four months. Hopefully she will have luck finding a job, since the country [Palestine] is a poor one and one has to struggle hard. She learned infant and child care. My oldest son, Shmiel [Sam], will travel to Palestine, God willing, as a tourist for four weeks to look around for a job. I'm curious to know how and what he'll achieve, since he will incur a lot of expenses. But, hopefully, it'll pay off. My sister-in-law, Cilli Kistenmacher has a boy, 16 years, and a girl of 12-13 years. A few days ago the

> Kistenmachers left for Buenos Aires with a heavy heart.

Six months later, on 1 September 1938, (18) my mother had good news to report. The affidavit for Simon had arrived, and there was great joy at home. "Dear Harry ... may all the good things that I wish for you come true ... I must point out again that he [Simon] is an educated, neat, very decent, mature young man, about which you will convince yourself. I am envied here for my well brought up children." But my mother's joy over Simon's assured immigration was overshadowed by her despair. There were still two more children at home for whom no immigration plans had been made. Nor had my mother allowed herself previously to express her own wish to escape herself with my father.

> I, too, would like to go to Palestine in spite of the very bad times, since there is nowhere else any opportunity ... we are 4 persons here. The girl [Betti], who will be 17 years old in two months, works in a household, and the boy [me] who will be 14 years is still in school. I have no idea how I can ever get out of here.

Barely two months later a cruel fate validated her despair.

The letter my mother wrote to Uncle Harry on 15 September 1938 (19) was her last letter from Hamburg. Highlighting the urgency of Simon's departure, she wrote that she would not wait for another five to six weeks for the Jewish committee to pay his fare. "We borrowed money wherever we could and sold our dining room to cover the travel expenses ... everything now goes topsy-turvy without any planning, and very quickly...." Simon wrote that he had received the visa from the American Consul, as well as passage on the S/S Manhattan, which would arrive in New York on 29 September at 9:00 a.m. Every hour, every week counted; a month later it would have been too late.

Simon (far left) with friends
S/S Manhattan 1938

4. Growing Up In Hamburg (1924-1938)

I was born the youngest of nine children, but the first to be delivered in a hospital, the Jewish Hospital in Hamburg. My father was 46 years old, and my mother, 39. I don't think it was a particularly joyful event for my virile father or for my exhausted mother, although she had the consoling thought that I would be the last of her brood. Indeed, I thought in my adult years that my having had to sleep between them in their bed when I was little might not have been entirely due to the lack of another bed. It may also have served as an effective form of birth control. I was a fat little baby with a very round head, a mop of black hair, and eyes that searched the surroundings with amazement. I believe I weighed over ten pounds at birth, and in those days that was thought to have been overweight and was a concern to my mother. Although I was never told anything about these earliest years of my life, I have come to believe that my feeding became an issue. For many years in my childhood I had a repetitive dream of being the last to be served at a meal, or finding that there was no food left for me. As an adult I tended to interpret these dreams as indications that I must have felt deprived. My mother was always very

Me at 3 Months

caring and attending to my needs; in fact, she soon became worried because as a growing child I was thin and a picky eater.

How did I get my name? I was not named after a deceased family member, as is the custom among Ashkenazi Jews. My parents must have run out of names by the time I arrived. A family by the name of Glattner, who had come from the Galician town of Przemysl, had two children, Heini and Rosi, who were close friends of my two older siblings. When Herr Glattner lay dying, he made my father promise to take care of his family. That vow proved to be quite unnecessary because my father, bon vivant that he was, concentrated much of his time and attention on the merry widow. My mother, no doubt, had her suspicions but kept them to herself. I was named after Herr Glattner.

"Gunther" never really suited me, but I was stuck with that name. ("Gunther" means warrior and is not an uncommon name in Germany.) In Britain I briefly considered changing it to Gerald, Gershwin, or Geoffrey, but I didn't like any one of them. My Hebrew name, "Gershom," on the other hand, fit me perfectly. It means "a stranger there" and is the name of the son of Moses. ("Gershon" is considered equivalent to Gershom by Biblical scholars, and is the name of Levi's oldest son.) I have always considered Gershom to be the Hebrew version of the Aramaic Gershon. Gershon was the name I was called by the Cornes of Cardiff. (More about them later.)

In 1924 our family lived in an apartment at Rentzelstrasse 5, in the Grindel area of Hamburg, where many Polish Jews had settled and had mixed with the resident German Jews. The first 5 years of my life are forever lost to me, except for a story about my brother Julius having saved my life after I had climbed onto (or had been left sitting on) the window ledge of our upstairs apartment. I had been looking out the open window onto the back yard when Julius saw me and pulled me back to safety. I cannot recall anything about that event. All I remember about that home is that we had gas lamps with very fragile elements that had to be replaced often. It was somehow fascinating to me.

Tragedy struck in 1929 when I was 5. My brother Isaac—we called him Edo—had graduated from high school (Talmud Tora, where all of us boys went) and was working as a deliveryman for our landlord who ran a tobacco business. He was driving a 3-wheeled van that was said to be unsafe when he and another vehicle collided. He died in the crash. My father was the first to learn of this fatal accident. He was in shock and kept Edo's death a secret from the rest of us for a while. My mother was devastated and depressed for a very long time. Edo was the apple of her eye; young, handsome, strong and, most important, he looked like my father when he wooed my mother during his courting days. I didn't know then of any of the circumstances of the accident, but I sensed the tragedy. All was quiet at home, unusually quiet. I will never forget the hush that fell over the house. It was the silence rather than an outcry that stayed with me and became my model for mourning.

My mother blamed the landlord and we moved out to another apartment, close by, at Grindelhof 8. It was also a move up for us. We now had electric light. We also had bedrooms for everyone in the family ... well, for everyone except me. The layout of the apartment was like a railroad sleeper car, with seven bedrooms off the long corridor, a dining room, a kitchen, and one bathroom. Yes, one bathroom. Our family now numbered nine—my parents, two adult children working outside the house, two teenage boys, and three school children. Since the routines of our daily life differed, we did not get in one another's way. My mother, Betti and I usually ate in the kitchen. Our mealtimes were adjusted to individual schedules, as my mother was always ready to wait on us. The dining room with its fine furniture, of course, was used only on special occasions and for Jewish holidays when we all ate together as a family.

I was five years old in 1929, and perhaps a little undernourished because I was a picky eater. Many times my mother sent me down the street to a dairy to have a cup of cream to fatten me up. I loved it. However, I was still underweight when my mother enrolled me in a summer camp for underprivileged (and perhaps also undernourished) Jewish children. It was called *Erholungsheim* (literally, "Recovery Home," essentially a rest cure), sustained by the three categorical imperatives of good health: Rest, Food, and Fresh Air. There were no particular activities that I can recall. After four weeks in the Rhineland Mountains we returned home by bus. Parents came to collect their children, and I waited to be picked up. But where was my mother? The place where we had assembled to wait had emptied out. Although a chaperone was with me, I felt alone.

At last, a woman came to get me. It was Frau Glattner, a family friend of ours, but I knew her only vaguely. She took me back to my mother who was at home, ill, and couldn't come to pick me up. That memory and the feeling of abandonment were formative in my emotional development. It was not the last time I felt that way.

At another time, much later, when I came home from school, I rang the doorbell, but did not get the usual prompt answer. I kept ringing harder and louder. Finally my mother appeared and opened the door. She was ill and had dragged herself out of bed to let me in. I felt as if I had hurt her badly. I have never forgotten it. Feeling guilty, for good reason or not, has ever been my weakness, perhaps from then on.

In this connection, I recall the impact that my favorite book (Stefan Zweig's "Die Augen des Ewigen Bruders") made on me when I was just a boy. Virata, the king's chief minister, surveys the enemy's casualties after his victorious battle and he comes across his slain brother whose eyes are open as if staring at him. Virata then commits himself to a just and harmless life. Young as I was, the story's theme resonated with me.

But I also felt undeserving and hesitant to make any demands, perhaps because of a sense that our family needed to keep our financial boat afloat. But in a small way, I benefitted from our having to buy food on credit. When I was sent to pay our monthly grocery bill, the grocer would give me a piece of chocolate. I always thought that happened because he was happy to get paid; it didn't occur to me that he just might have liked me or was simply being kind to a little boy.

Meanwhile, outside the confines of my little world, the Nazis were gaining and demonstrating their power. Because Hamburg was Germany's "window to the world" the persecution of Jews was relatively contained, at least for the time we were still there. However, "unrests" took place in and around Hamburg. In his well-known and well-documented treatise on Nazi Germany, Walter Shirer recorded that "On Sunday, July 10 [1932], 18 persons were done to death in the streets, and on the following Sunday, when the Nazis under police escort staged a march through Altona, a working class suburb of Hamburg, nineteen persons were shot to death and 285 wounded." This was known as 'The Altona Riots." Such bloody skirmishes may or may not have been published in the local paper (perhaps unless they showed the Nazi's prowess), but our family's concern was about events in our neighborhood. We, too, saw street fights between the Nazis on one side and the Communists and Social Democrats on the other. And I watched some of those street battles from the safety of our balcony before Hitler came to power in 1933.

We belonged to the Social Democrats—at least my brothers did—and we had the "Drei Pfeile" ("Three Arrows") flag hanging from the balcony over the objections of our frightened, nonpolitical parents. Our family friends, the four brothers Schainowsky, card-carrying communists, joined the Social Democrats in taking on the Nazis in the street, but they were out-numbered. In one of the street skirmishes the Schainowskys, chased by the Nazis, came running up to our second floor apartment for safety. The Nazis did not pursue them further, but we all remained very, very cautious. Later, three of the Schainowsky brothers, brilliant at chess, proved their expert maneuvering skills by outwitting the Germans in their escape from the country. Theirs is a story worthy of a Hollywood movie.

My home, my school, and our synagogue were the pillars of my life and the boundaries of my world. Our synagogue, the *Neue Dammtor* Synagoge, which we called the "Benecke shul" ("Benecke" was the name of the street, which no longer exists) was built at the end of an alley at a time when it was important not to flaunt Jewish buildings. It was a relatively modest structure but quite beautiful, hidden from passers-by. Ultimately, however, its secluded location did not ensure its survival. On my return visit to Hamburg many years later I saw a little memorial stone that had been erected where the shul stood, and that, too, remained hid-den behind some bushes. Hamburg's main synagogue, just a few houses down the street from us, was an architectural masterpiece, which served the more orthodox and affluent members of our community. That

Benecke Shul

Hamburg's Main Synagogue (as it looked in 1908)

synagogue was totally torched during Kristallnacht. There is now a memorial plaque on the far side of the now-empty space, totally unadorned.

My school, Talmud Tora Realschule, was just a block down the street, and our synagogue was just around the corner from our apartment. A kosher butcher, grocery stores, a Hebrew bookstore, other small businesses; all were on our block on Grindelhof, a side street of Grindelallee, the main thoroughfare. There was also a shop next to our house whose sole business was running wet wash through its mangle. My mother did the family laundry in our apartment, bending over to rub every piece of clothing or linen on her washboard. We would carry the load of wet bed sheets downstairs to get them wrung out through the shop's rollers; *i.e.*, the mangle. Then we had to carry the flattened load back up to our apartment and hang it all out to dry. Just another chore for my mother and me. I remember farther down at the end of the Grindelallee, at an intersection called "Schlump," was a tobacconist where I bought my dad a cigar for his 60th birthday using my own savings. (Although I did not get a weekly allowance, I must have been able to save a few pfennige here and there.)

Talmud Tora Realschule
Survived Unscathed, 1949

I have many memories from my school days at Talmud Tora. I started going to Talmud Tora Realschule in 1930 when I was almost 6 years old. It had no kindergarten. For the first day in school all the boys—no girls at Talmud Tora—arrived with a cone like a cornucopia, filled with candies and chocolates to sweeten the separation from home, and to symbolize the fruits of learning. But I wonder—did my mother really have the money to send me off with such a filled cone so I would not feel different from the other kids? Whenever possible she would make sure that I would have no reason to feel self-conscious. Going to a Jewish day school had many advantages. We school kids had no classes on any Jewish holidays or on the national holidays. But we crammed both a secular curriculum and our religious studies into a five-day school week. And most important of all, we were in a safe environment, protected from Nazi harass-ment and, later, from the edict of making German schools "Judenrein."

My Cousin Margot With Cornucopia

I was very shy and nearsighted. When the teacher would write something on the blackboard, I would have to go right up to it to read what he wrote, and that was embarrassing. I was timid and self-conscious in class, but I loved to learn. My first grade teacher was Herr Meyer. We used to sing "Shalom

Rabbi Meyer, shalom ..." when he entered the room, and he would answer us with his sweet voice in like manner: "Shalom yeladim (children), shalom ...." In his alphabetized attendance record I was, of course, the last pupil (with the name Zloczower) and, somehow, was missed when the report cards were handed out at the end of the first year. But never mind. Herr Meyer stopped by our house and hand delivered my report card to my parents, telling them that I was a good student and had a brain like a sponge: I absorbed well, but had to be squeezed to yield the learned material.

The school discipline was very strict, typical of German pedagogy. We had to stand up whenever a teacher entered a classroom and wait for him to give us a signal to sit down. One teacher noticed that I tended to tilt my head slightly to the right. My head was evidently a little out of line with the others in my row. Well, with his stentorian voice he commanded me "lower that left ear." I did. I sat down. And no talking in class at any time. Herr Meyer, who taught in the lower grade levels, was clearly a more lenient teacher, perhaps an exception. Another teacher I had, however, was more typical. He used numbers or, more correctly, uttered numbers to maintain control in the class. When he said *"eins,"* (one) we were warned to be quiet and attentive. When he said *"zwei,"* (two) he signaled that he was already getting angry and we could expect physical punishment for the slightest misbehavior. It never came to *"drei."* (three). Any wonder? (I might say in this connection that my brother Julius later told me that some of his teachers were even more abusive than those whom I had experienced.) I was very conforming, never really got into any trouble, and yet I did not entirely escape the wrath of one teacher. One day a slap across my face sent my glasses flying across the room. The offense? I don't know any more, but it didn't happen again. All our teachers at Talmud Tora were Jewish, with one exception: the gym teacher. Were no Jewish gym teachers available? It certainly reflected an element in Jewish tradition that valued intellectual over physical education. Nonetheless, I did like gymnastics and track. I liked to run and jump, tackle the parallel bars and the pommel horse. But the rings were not for me.

Like boys everywhere, we made fun of our teachers, complained about our homework, and enjoyed our recess. The school's backyard was our playground. In the schoolyard, we played "schlagball" with a ball made from the stiff wax paper in which our lunch had been wrapped. I don't recall the rules, but I remember that we would hit the paper with an open hand. I loved that game. For another game we used our pocket knives. We drew a line on the ground and flipped the knife from knee height, trying to get the knife to stick in the ground. Whoever stuck the knife right on the line or closest to it, won. And then there was a game we played with 5 metal dice (cubes with blank sides). We played this game on a smoothened patch of ground. The player would throw one die in the air, quickly snatch another from the flat ground, and then catch the thrown die before it dropped. He would next toss up the two dice in his hand and pick up another from the ground, then go on to try with three, four, and five dice. This actually took some skill, and I was pretty good at it.

The German school system was and still is, I believe, distinctly different from the British and American systems. In our Jewish parochial school, we started with Hebrew as well as German in the first grade, and had religious and secular classes in all subsequent grades. The first through fourth grades corresponded to the American elementary school, but at the end of the fourth year, our curriculum divided into two tracks: academic and vocational. The fifth grade class was already the beginning of my "high school," called the *"Unterquarta"*, and there I started my first English class. Entering the *Unterquarta* I got my school cap, a green cap with a visor and a silver band. It was a gift from my parents. I wore it proudly and it became my prized possession. My next year's class was the *"Oberquarta"* (Upper Fourth) with the addition of French to my German, Hebrew, and English classes. With this promotion I could now replace the silver band on my cap for a gold one.

To my lasting regret, the Jewish subjects were not my favorites. I liked languages. Hebrew was not taught conversationally, but the better to understand Torah and the prayers. French appealed to me because it is melodic and regular. I would always study my French lessons well ahead of the assignment, and I dreamed of going to France one day. To boost my English, I used to "borrow" (without his knowledge) my older brother Sam's English language magazines, to which he subscribed, and study the section on idiomatic expressions. I think that is how I got a feel for conversational English before I had an opportunity to speak the language. I had advanced to the next level, the

"Untertertia" (Lower Third), and had set my sights on learning the classical languages, when fate stopped my formal education in 1938.

During my school years I was pretty much protected from the Nazi whirlwind that drew Germany's Jews into an ever-deepening abyss. I felt safe at home and at school, and I did not venture out beyond our Grindel, our neighborhood. I was raised with clear constraints. We Jewish children were expected to be quiet, well behaved, and conforming. I remember the day I was walking home from synagogue with my father, and kicked some stones in the street just for fun. He admonished me with: "A Jewish boy doesn't do that." The values we lived by rarely had to be made explicit. Needless to say we didn't hang around anywhere in public; we watched our step.

As more and more Jewish families left Hamburg (1935-1938) our class sizes continued to shrink and an ambience of temporariness befell our school, symbolized by the empty seats of our former classmates. At many moments we were glancing around to see who might be the next to leave. A friend of mine went with his family to the Netherlands, and I corresponded with him for a time. I don't know what happened to him. Neither did I know what happened to my beloved Talmud Tora Schule after I left (involuntarily) in late 1938. I was saddened to learn on a return visit to Hamburg in 1973 that the Nazis had taken over both Jewish schools in Hamburg. They converted my school to a vocational school for German youth, while the girls' school on the Carolinen Strasse absorbed the remaining Jewish boys that were transferred from the Talmud Tora. In 1940 or 1941, the Nazis shipped off all the boys and girls that remained in the *Judische Tochter Schule*, together with their teachers, to extermination camps.

The general atmosphere at home was rather grim. As Nazi edicts made life for Jews increasingly unbearable, we made do with little hope or joy. The hardships created tension among us. I remember hearing only serious talk at home, lots of complaints and worries, and little laughter. My mother's daily routines consisted of work, sacrifice, and self-denial, with periodic relief only on Shabbat, on our festivals and Holy Days. She worked from early dawn into the night, cleaning the apartment, cooking everything from scratch, hand-washing the linen, and looking after us kids. She had no days off or nights out, and refused to leave the house for a weekend escape. Yet she visited regularly an old acquaintance, Frau Gewurtz, who lived in a nursing home. It was a *mitzvah* to ease that woman's loneliness, and Frau Gewurtz repaid my mother's compassion by knitting two *yarmulkes* for me, which I gave to my son, Ed, who will pass them on to his son, Ari.

Chess offered some relief. I always hung around Sam and Simon when they played chess with their friends (usually the Schainowsky boys or Heini Glattner). I could not have been older than six when I first learned to play. Julius, too, played chess but he was not in Sam or Simon's league. They were very serious about chess, often played for money, and they studied the strategies of masters. I never studied chess systematically as they did, and never developed my game. However, when I was 14 I took part in the German Junior Chess Maccabiah and placed 5th, for which I got a tie as a prize. My mother made me give the tie to my brother Julius. She said boys did not wear ties, and I didn't need it. I did not mind. In our family everything was judged on the basis of "need."

I was nine years old in 1933 when Hitler came to power, and soon after, the open discrimination and persecution of Jews led to joblessness and loss of business among Jews. My father, who lost his furniture store during the Depression, was at the time a traveling salesman, but the Nazis put an end to that. (Who would buy from a Jew?) All he could do then was to take a job as a laborer on the Hamburg docks, rolling oil barrels from the pier to the loading platform. And that miserable job he got only with Sam's pull. (Sam still had an important position at HAPAG—a venerable Hamburg-based shipping company—for which the Nazis exempted him.) On Papa's way home from work, tired and reeking of oil, he used to pass by the Hamburg fairgrounds ("Hamburger Dom") and pick up some candy to bring home for me. I waited for him. When he arrived home and relaxed on the sofa, I brought my chess set and tried to teach him how to play. This was my first paid enterprise; I got a few pfennige for every lesson.

The ever-increasing Nazi edicts restricted Jews on all levels of human affairs, and began destroying our family's normal life, as my mother described in a letter of 24 April 1933 (20) to Uncle Harry. Cilli typed that letter so that my mother's message would be perfectly clear:

> The boycott [of Jewish businesses] lasted only one day, everything else in

> Hamburg remained rather quiet. For the most part all [Jewish] newspapers are banned, and what you hear [meaning, what one hears] is totally one-sided. Kosher meat is also banned, and so we have no meat. But one thing is clear: we few Jews will now band together more closely than before because only sorrow unites.

My mother believed in the redeeming effect of suffering.

My mother's claim in her April 1933 letter that "we were not much affected" (by the political events) was no longer true a year later. Her next letter of 3 November 1937 (21) showed how the Nazi noose was tightening. Work opportunities and existing employment for Jews were shut down. Economic life for us became desperate:

> My husband has been unemployed for 3 years, which is not exactly news. My oldest daughter, Cilli, who has been married for 5 years, is in Trieste [Italy]. Her husband has gone to sea on a boat plying between Haifa and Trieste. Cilli went there so her husband could be with her and their child every 14 days when the ship was in harbor. They have no bread...my oldest son Shmuel [Sam] is still working in his business, earns well but must support the house [expenses], as well as Cilli in Trieste ....

By this time my Aunt Cilli's family on my father's side was no better off. "Do you remember Cilli, Chaim's sister," my mother wrote:

> [T]hey had 2 big shops selling eggs. They did very well, but now it is 2 years that they have lost their business ... they live from their savings. How long can that last? One can die ... he, his wife, one big son age 16 and a girl of 12 are breaking down ... to be a Jew and suffer the discrimination is very hard to bear... I fearfully tremble that the business where Sam is employed does not go kaput, because then we can go begging ... the youngest three are still in school. The youngest, Gunther, is a bright boy, a good student ....

My mother did not burden me, however, with her worries about our survival. I may have overheard the adults discussing the deteriorating situation, but I grew up with the admonition that children are to be seen and not heard. I devoted myself solely to my schoolwork, but I was neither a bookworm nor a nerd. A picture from the family album attests to my other, equal talent for taking it easy. Although I was friendly with several kids in my class, I never had a close or best friend. Nor did I get together with anyone outside of class. I was very shy, and ashamed of our family being poor, so I never invited anyone to our house.

Unlike some of my brothers and sisters, however, I did not mind that our parents usually spoke Yiddish, although they certainly knew German well. And I was not embarrassed by my parents' East European manners; they didn't have to be models of acculturation. At the risk of sounding as if I were my parents' pet, I would say that I loved my parents

Me, Age 13, Relaxing At Home In Hamburg, 1938

unambivalently, and I was protective rather than critical of them. I felt particularly protective of my dad who was at times the object of my older brothers' disdain. In fact, I remember an incident that yields an insight into the kind of kid I was. My dad once broke open my piggy bank and took the money I had saved. My mother was furious, but I never felt hurt or deprived. I felt sorry for my dad who evidently needed the money. It didn't matter to me what he needed the money for.

By the mid-1930's, Jewish children in Germany were not allowed to go to any German school. We accepted two Jewish boys, Milo (whose last name I can't recall) and Emil Sabielak from other parts of Germany, to stay with us and attend our Talmud Tora. Their parents paid for their board, which helped us out. They were close in age to Edith and Betti and became fast friends with my sisters. Betti's love for Emil was steadfast. Emil later made it to England and, when I was leaving for England in 1939, Betti repeatedly asked me to contact him and give him her regards. Her adolescent love for Emil was pure, but went unanswered. I wrote to Emil from Cardiff, but he was married by then, and I could not forgive him for what I naively felt was his betrayal of Betti.

My sisters and their in-house boyfriends spent much time together, while I watched—and daydreamed—at a distance. I had reached my teen years and had become interested in girls. The boys in our school advertised their interest, but I'm not sure I did. They would place straight pins with different color heads in the lapel of their jackets to indicate whether they had girlfriends or were looking. I probably thought that if I had displayed pins on my jacket no girl would respond. Our school was strictly for boys, and whatever occasions may have existed for co-educational mixing, I avoided. Once I was invited to two Bar Mitzvah parties on the same day. By the time I could gather enough courage to go to one, the kids weren't expecting me any longer and I began looking for a gracious way to escape only moments after I had arrived. That remained one of my most mortifying memories.

My own Bar Mitzvah took place in October 1937 on the Shabbat closest to my 13th birthday according to the Jewish calendar. It came after the end of the Succoth holiday, and was a modest affair, nothing like contemporary American productions. However, many in our congregation came to the synagogue to celebrate the occasion with their presence. Following *Simchat Torah,* which is the last day of Succoth, the weekly Shabbat Torah readings start a new annual cycle from the beginning of the Torah (Genesis). That October Shabbat I was called up to chant a portion of the Torah, (a *parshah* of Genesis, 5:27-31). In spite of my trembling self-consciousness, my soprano voice came across loud and clear, and made my family very proud of me. My passage states that Methusalem lived 969 years (a still arguable event in the Bible) and the chanting of this *parshah* requires a most unusual intonation that I can still sing. Unlike some other boys who were more ambitious or more religious, I did not chant the entire *parshah* on that Shabbat, nor did I read the "*Haftorah.*" How I secretly envied those boys! After I chanted my portion I returned to my seat next to my Papa, much relieved, and waited for the end of the Torah service.

The conspicuous place in front of the Holy Ark was awesome and intimidating enough when I had to stand on the *bimah* and chant my Torah portion. But later, after the Torah service, I had to stand there a second time for the whole congregation to watch, as our rabbi addressed me in his sermon. I stood like a soldier at attention on the *bimah* and, to all appearances, listened to what the rabbi had to say. I didn't really hear or remember a word he said, but I

SYNAGOGE AN DER BENECKESTRASSE
The Bimah At Benecke Shul

am sure he must have exhorted me to continue my Jewish education and remain faithful to the Jewish tradition. Did he include a word of warning in his address to the congregation about the vulnerability of our life as Jews in Nazi Germany? Did he know what might have been in the offing? These were not my questions then. It was just an ordinary Bar Mitzvah, when the outside world was forgotten for just a few hours.

After the services several congregation members came over to our house to congratulate my parents and me, to partake of the honey cake my mother had baked, and to have a shot of my father's best "*bronfen.*" There were "mazel tovs" all around. I had joined the ranks of Jewish men and was entitled to all the privileges provided in the prayer service, but I also was expected to attend daily services to help meet the required quorum of 10 adults ("*minyan*"). Early in the morning before going to school, I accompanied my dad down the street and around the corner to our little shul, where we were always heartily welcomed by the "regulars," who were waiting for us to complete the *minyan* before beginning the prayers.

I got three presents for my Bar Mitzvah that are very precious to me and which I still have: a modern silk *tallit* from Sam that he had brought back from his last trip to London, a green velvet tallit bag from my mother which she had embroidered painstakingly with my Hebrew initials on one side and with a Magen David on the other, and a pocket Siddur, (an incredible 3 in. x 4½ in. edition with German translations) from Herr van der Zyl, which he had Simon inscribe. Herr van der Zyl was a small, old Jewish veteran from World War I, a lodger in our house, who regaled me with stories about his soldiering for the Second German Reich. He had no way of knowing, of course, that even if he had won an Iron Cross medal in that war, it would not have saved him from Hitler's "Final Solution."

Like my older brothers, I belonged to the shul choir and spent the best part of the services in the upper balcony where our choral voices wafted down to the assembled congregation below. Men were on the main floor and the women on the lower balcony. I was the lead soprano in the front row, near the choir director, where I was exposed to his vigorous gesticulations. He was a fat little man with great ambitions, who sweated profusely and sprinkled me with droplets at every fortissimo. He took the choir rehearsals very seriously, but I can't say that the rest of us did. The male tenors and basses used to look down at the women's balcony and make risqué jokes. I must admit I, too, looked furtively at the girls in their fine dresses as my mind sinfully wandered from the prayer book. When I got down from the choir, I would go sit next to my father in the pews. He could always follow the service (all in Hebrew) perfectly and find the right place in the prayer book for me so I could catch up with the speedy *chasan*. I was proud of my Papa.

The Jewish holidays at home were my most joyful times and have always provided the most bittersweet memories in my nostalgic reveries. Preparing for *Pesach* was the most exciting of them all. As traditional Jews we kept kosher; we had separate sets of dishes for dairy and for meat, and I would observe the custom of maintaining the prescribed times between eating the *milchig* and the *fleishig* food. For Passover we had two other sets of dishes that we did not use at any other time, as required by our tradition. After my mother had cleaned the kitchen of all *chometz*, we brought our *Pesach* dishes down from the attic to replace our everyday bowls, plates, cups and saucers. But we had no special pots and pans for this holiday. We had to use the everyday cookware, which had to be made kosher for *Pesach*. That procedure was great fun. My mother took the big tin tub, in which she had once probably bathed the babies, filled it with cold water and put all the pots and pans in it. Then she heated a flat iron on the kitchen stove until it was red hot and dropped it in the tub, which turned the tub into a steaming and sizzling cauldron. How I loved to watch that. (It was also a very busy time for me because I would hang around my mother, trying to help.) The coal range on which my mother cooked had removable concentric rings of cast iron to regulate the heat. No electric or gas oven then, at least not in our apartment.

The best part of Pesach was, of course, the Seder. My mother would buy a live carp from the fish store the night before the Seder and deposit it in our bathtub.

The next day she would kill it and make gefilte fish. She would save the head for my father who, to my amazement, considered it his favorite part of the fish. That evening our whole family would assemble at the table in the rarely used dining room, an event that brought Sam, Simon, Julius and me together for a choral performance. Each of my brothers had been in the shul choir in his time, and we all knew the songs. We would all sing in harmony, with Julius taking alto. Our breaking into song would provide a welcome pause during my father's machine-gun style reading of the *Haggada*. I am not sure, however, that he understood all the Hebrew he was rattling off. Like all Jews at the seder, any time, anywhere, we wanted to get to the meal my mother had carefully prepared ... to enjoy finally all the traditional dishes and the gefilte fish she had made from scratch.

We needed a lot of matzot for our Seder and the eight days of Pesach, but we couldn't afford to buy them at the local Jewish grocery store. So Julius would borrow a flat-bed cart, and he and I would load up the cart with dozens of matzo boxes from a community matzo distribution center. I remember well how Julius would pull the cart with me perched on top, holding the stacked boxes to keep them from falling off.

The High Holidays were, of course, very special and strictly observed. When the Days of Awe were ushered in I became very conscious of my behavior, even though I was far from taking the admonitions and godly punishments seriously. That was the time when I would wear my best clothes, and my mother would take time out to go shul with the rest of us.

Every *chasan* in our community was judged by his operatic power, and every rabbi's reputation was based on the erudition of his sermons. Young as I was, I was very moved by the *Kol Nidrei*, by the list of ways in which we might die, by the benedictions, and by the pleas for redemption that highlighted my prayers. I loved the songs, their passionate melodies and their ancient text. The fasting mandated for Yom Kippur was a matter of pride for us kids; we competed with one another. Who could hold out the longest without eating or drinking? I was allowed to break the fast already in the early afternoon, because my mother was forever worried about my health.

A happier holiday was Succoth, which my family celebrated in the *sukkah* erected adjacent to our shul. We had neither the space nor the money to build our own *sukkah.* There I got to shake the *lulav* with an *etrog* in my hands in every direction: east, west, north, south, up and down, signifying that God is everywhere. I enjoyed all the Jewish rituals and felt how meaningful, even necessary, they must have been to faithful Jews throughout the ages. I never abided by those revisionists who would not honor what they deemed outmoded. Succoth was my harbinger, not only for more fun and celebrations, but also for my birthday, just days away.

5. Our Deportation From Hamburg To Zbaszyn (1938 – 1939)

It was on 28 October 1938, at 6:00 o'clock in the morning that a loud, insistent knock on our door awoke us. We were still in bed when we heard the unmistakable command, *"Mach schnell! Raus!"* (*Hurry up! Get out!*). Papa and Sam got up, hastily donned pants, and opened the door. Facing them were two uniformed S.A. or S.S. men who stated that we were all under arrest. Why? "No questions asked, just do what we tell you. Get your clothes on and come with us. You have 15 minutes." Where were they taking us? What was this all about? But we asked no more questions. We knew there would be no answers. Papa, Mutti, Sam, Betti and I got ready. Should we take anything with us? There was no time, nor did we know just what to take. As we gathered by the door, one of the Nazi officers pointed at me, "*Nicht Du!*" (Not you!). He told me I could not go with my parents; he was arresting only adults and children over 16. Betti was almost 17. Then she, along with Sam and my parents simply disappeared. There was no good-bye. I was now totally on my own.

I was bewildered, confused, panicky. What should I do? To go to school that morning didn't even occur to me. I ran downstairs into the street as if I could find some sign or direction. I impulsively turned into the street around the corner where the Kistenmachers lived. Surely my uncle and aunt would be able to help me, I thought. I rang their bell, but nobody came to answer the door. Were they afraid to open the door? Or had they, too, been arrested and taken away? My mind went numb. I ran back out into the street aimlessly. As luck would have it, there was another Jewish boy looking lost in the street. I didn't know him, but we immediately bonded: his parents had been taken away, too. Finding an ally in this nightmare helped my panic ease up a little. We decided to turn ourselves in to the police in the hope that they might help us find our parents. We walked to the police station. "Arrest us, too" we pleaded. A desperate request that the Nazi police were only too glad to oblige.

Little did we know then that all 16,000 Polish Jews in Germany had been rounded up that day and the night before, for deportation to Poland. The Nazis had ordered this hasty deportation in response to Poland's announcement requiring all Polish citizens living outside the country to return to Poland by 31 October 1938 to maintain their citizenship. Many Polish Jews (like our family) had been living in Germany for decades and had no intention of, or means for, returning to Poland. Hitler did not want Germany's Polish Jews to lose their Polish citizenship because that would have rendered them stateless and placed them under the protection of the League of Nations, the forerunner of the United Nations.

The other boy and I were taken to a huge, crowded assembly area outside the Altona railroad station. The sun was at its height, but did not warm the chilly autumn air. Men, women, children, young and old, all were massed into this open space; suddenly homeless, helpless, and heaven-abandoned people. With the world they knew already destroyed, they were fearful of their fate. The police brought me to this overcrowded assembly. But how could I possibly find my parents and Betti? And how could the police know where they were? My anguish was soon allayed. How I was reunited with my parents and Betti in this assembly of hapless humanity I will never know. The memory of the moment of my reunion with my parents is completely lost to me. I have always regarded it as a miracle ... and not the last one I would experience in this phase of my life.

We were ordered to board the train, hundreds of us. Not cattle cars, but only just enough room for everyone. Ah, German efficiency. Where were we headed? How long would it take to wherever we were bound? How the unknown haunted us. Were we headed for a camp? Was death awaiting us? Our mind went in circles. We traveled through the night, sleepless and shaken, destination unknown. When our train finally came to a stop in the morning, we were ordered to get off and start walking. Where were we? We had arrived at a small station, seemingly out in an open field with no village or any signs of life in sight.

"Man los! Schnell!" (Get going! Hurry up!) German soldiers who had come along as guards were chasing us like cowboys herding cattle. We kept in line, heads downcast, there was no end in sight. What a pathetic procession of men, women, and children, some carrying bundles or old suitcases, all trotting along as best as their legs would carry them, as if moved by an invisible force. My parents, Betti and I had nothing to carry; yet we were weighed down with a heavy load of fear and numbness. There was only one way to go—forward—and we finally saw where we were headed. It had taken us a long time,

perhaps hours. There in the open field were border gates that marked the very end of German territory and the beginning of "no-man's land," an empty tract of uncultivated land between Germany and Poland.

The German soldiers—they may have been S.A. or S.S.—herded us to the frontier and opened the border gates. Like cattle driven into their pens, we were pushed into this no-man's land, about the size of two football fields. There was no looking back, let alone moving back; the Nazis saw to that. On this tract of cursed earth, the trainload of thousands of us crowded together as if our closeness could protect us from our feared fate. Was this the end of our trek? Or the end of our lives? We were hemmed in, helpless. With the German border behind us, perhaps we could at least cross over onto Polish soil. Oh no, not yet. The Polish border guards on the other side had orders not to let us into Polish territory! This must have been a trap! There was no escape and nowhere to hide.

The German soldiers had not yet completed their mission. We were not yet on Polish soil, and the Nazis probably thought that some of us might be so foolhardy or desperate as to run or sneak back into Germany. Well, there was only one thing for them to do: The armed Nazis mounted their bayonets and started firing. They fired in the air, but we didn't know that. All hell broke loose. People began to panic and scream and cry. What happened then seems unreal to me now. Looking towards the unyielding border, I saw the Polish guards, perhaps three or more, each holding on to someone, so I figured they would not let go of their charges to chase after me. Disregarding my family and the risk I was taking, I ran for my life across the Polish border and immediately took shelter in the doorway of the empty guardhouse. I heard the shooting amid the shouting and crying as I cringed and pressed myself against the entrance wall of the guardhouse. I was a terrified observer of the scene, alone and in mortal danger. But not for long. The border was breached and I saw waves of panicked people come streaming across, my parents and Betti among them! How could I have possibly found them in this maelstrom? Since the only path from no-man's land into Poland was past the guardhouse, I must have seen them running by. That was my second miracle: as if by magic, I again was suddenly reunited with my parents. Now, 75 years later, I wonder: was it a myth I have created?

We had been through hell, yet came through alive. Together again, we kept walking along with thousands of other exhausted deportees, hoping to find some sign of civilization. We finally came to a village by the name of Zbaszyn, pronounced Zbonshin, or Bentschen in German. (That is ironic—or prophetic—because the word "bentschen" is Yiddish for "praying"). Even before we entered the village, rumors were flying about what might happen to us. Some were the most foreboding of possibilities, others were fantasies of rescue and freedom. One such rumor was that, on our arrival at the railroad station, a train would come and take us into the interior of Poland. We would not have to stay in this God-forsaken village. Zbaszyn had a small train station, not much larger than a Metro stop with a waiting room, furnished with a plain bench and a wooden table. We were packed in, and waited, and waited. And waited. Most people spent the night on their feet because there was no room for anyone to move or to sit down. I was the lucky one, probably because I was just a kid; I had the table to stretch out on ... for two nights running. That is how long it took for us to realize that no train would be coming, we would have to find some accommodations in the village.

We didn't know it at the time but we were pawns in Poland's negotiations with Germany. Poland had invalidated our passports and was trying to keep us out, while Germany would not accept anyone returning. So the Poles kept us herded in a provisional ghetto. Zbaszyn, a village with 5,400 residents (including 52 Jews!) was simply overwhelmed by us at a ratio of two to one. As the crowd at the train station dispersed, everyone was trying to find a place to stay. My parents, Betti and I wandered through the village streets searching for a place to stay, but all available accommodations were quickly taken up. However, on the very edge of the village we found a farmhouse, run by a woman and her daughter. They were willing to rent us their spare room. The room was completely bare, but we were grateful to be able to sleep on the straw mattresses that the woman provided. Her name was Pana Szczecinska (pronounced Shchetshinska). She was a kindly woman, clearly worn out from her hard work and looking much older than her age. She had compassion for us, but had little else to offer. I remember she had a sore on her thumb, which I dressed with the first aid kit I had with me. Grateful and impressed with my caring for her thumb, she predicted that I would become a doctor one day.

(Yes, I did, but not a medical one.) I watched her young daughter running and frolicking on the farm, and I wanted to play with her. The girl threw a few glances at me. But I could not bring myself to break the Talmudic injunction not to fraternize with non-Jews. Or was my orthodox excuse a cover for my shyness?

The memory of my having treated Pana Szczecinska's sore thumb leads me back to an earlier experience. The week before our deportation I had suffered from boils on my body (like the 6th plague) and had gone to the Jewish hospital clinic to have them lanced. My Papa was with me for support. I remember that people in the waiting room, German Jews, were berating Polish Jews, saying "good riddance." Perhaps they knew what was in the offing for us. But little did they anticipate a fate even worse than ours. While we initially were deported to Poland, they later would be shipped directly to the concentration camps. When my medical procedure was over, I got that first aid kit, and my Papa stopped on the way home and bought me a beer. (There was no age restriction.) This was a rare moment with my dad, which I will not forget: he had validated my coming of age.

An historical aside that I also must record is that our crowd of deportees in Zbaszyn included a middle-aged couple by the name of Grynszpan who had experienced the same horrors that we had. They had written a despairing letter to their 19-year-old son, Hershel, who was living illegally in Paris. Alarmed and vengeful, Hershel took a gun to the German embassy, intending to kill the ambassador. But an official, Ernst vom Rath, came to the door. Hershel shot and mortally wounded vom Rath, who died in a Paris hospital 2 days later. This assassination provided Goebbels with an excuse to launch a pogrom of Jews all over Germany and Austria that he had planned previously. This abominable pogrom became known as the infamous Kristallnacht, which signaled to the world that the Nazi destruction of Jews was going into high gear. But it also mobilized British Jewry to organize the Refugee Children's Movement that rescued Jewish children from Germany and from Poland to safety in Great Britain. It arranged a seemingly instantaneous, intricate connection between of these little victims with their guardians in England, known as the "Kindertransport." I was one of them.

When we were still cooped up in the tiny railroad station in Zbaszyn, an agent from the Refugee Children's Movement came to enroll children up to the age of 16 for the Kindertransport. My mother did not hesitate for a moment, thinking if the Refugee Children's Movement would make good on its promise, it would be a miracle from heaven. But she was too honest to get Betti on that list. Betti had just turned 17! Fortunately, relief organizations came quickly to Zbaszyn, setting up soup kitchens, medical facilities, an information center and postal services. Life on a physical level was endurable. We could survive and stay in touch with Sam in England, Cilli, Julius, Edith in Palestine, and Simon in the U.S. My brothers and sisters sent us money, whatever they could afford, and tried to get us the necessary papers to emigrate. Most importantly, they supported our hope to get out of Poland and live again a normal life in their midst. For my parents and Betti that was not to be.

Life in Zbaszyn for the next 9 months was like being in a refugee camp under siege, uncertain and primitive, but not life-threatening. The Polish police had cordoned off the entire village, and our farmhouse was just outside the area limits. Most of the time we were holed up in our room, but could slip into the village. Whenever one of us had to go get food supplies or mail—luckily the mail got through—we had to sneak by the guards. During the day this was not much of a problem; we could see the guard, talk to him, and he would let us cross. At nighttime, however, this was risky; another guard might not recognize us as harmless refugees. When there was a knock on the door at night our hearts jumped. Fortunately we were neither hurt nor harassed. We got by, thanks to the relief organizations and the help of our family overseas. But we still had a taste of Polish anti-Semitism.

In a letter to Uncle Harry, my mother wrote on 12 February 1939, (22):

> In Poland everything is probably much cheaper, but the hate of Jews leads every day to fights with Jews in spite of the police ban. I'll tell you a little incident so you can get the picture. We had to go register and, since our name starts with "Z" [the last in line] it happened that we got to register only just before 10 p.m. when it closes. The people [officials] here crawl, they are so slow; it took 3

weeks to get the registration done [presumably because it took that long to get through the alphabet.] When Chaim [my father] was on his way home two guys approached him and hit him on the head. Thank God, it was not very bad. His hat flew off. He was not prepared for such a thing and, moreover, he was tired from standing around all day. He came home all broken up after a half hour in the wind and the rain. This is what happens to many here. Some make reports [to the police], but who knows who these hooligans are?

My mother wrote to Sam (in England), Simon (in the U.S), Cilli, Julius, and Edith (in Palestine), to file papers for our immigration. We hoped that at least one country would allow us to enter. We need not have asked, because my brothers and sisters already were besieging the respective authorities with applications for our immigration. Simon's desperate attempt to get us affidavits for the U. S. could not be processed because the Polish quota was filled, and we were given no hope of getting a visa any time soon. Neither was there a way to get the necessary certificate to come to Palestine. We were stuck, and had to set our sights on getting at least to Lwow, deeper into Poland. Perhaps we could live in Lwow, my father's hometown, where we still had some family. Uncle Munio, his wife and children lived in Lwow, but we had been totally out of touch with him and his family for many years. What a surprise it must have been for him to get a letter from us, telling him that we were in Zbaszyn and were hoping to come to Lwow when they let us out.

6. From Zbaszyn To Lwow And Otwock (1939)

Free at last! The day finally came in August 1939 that the Polish government relented and allowed us to leave Zbaszyn for the interior of Poland. It didn't take us long to pack (we had very little) and get to the railroad station, bound for Lwow. It was a long distance, perhaps over 400 miles diagonally across Poland, a long ride filled with relief from ghetto-like life and apprehension about the future. Yet during that trip we were mostly silent. Were we already trying to forget our most recent experience? Or were we reluctant to express our hidden doubts about our future? I for one must have been again in a daze.

We broke the trip at a small town called Grodek Jagielonsky, not far from Lwow, and stayed that night in a flea-bitten hotel. I imagine Betti might have made fun of it, since that would have been so much like her. That night I looked out of the hotel window and saw the storm clouds that blackened the town square. It looked foreboding. I thought the end of the world had come. But my fatigue and weariness overcame my anxiety about the storm and I soon fell asleep. The next morning we continued our trip.

My memory of our arrival and of my brief stay in Lwow is very clouded. It was overwhelming for me to register, let alone absorb, the names and faces and goings-on that I encountered. Nor was there any time for me to adjust to all these changes, or to find reassurance in my parents' outwardly calm behavior. I have no doubt that our new-old relatives on my father's side warmly welcomed and accommodated us. Back in Hamburg we had little contact with the Schneider (Uncle Munio's) family, but that changed with our arrival in Lwow. What I have come to know about my Uncle Munio, with whom I had spent so little time when we shared his home for two weeks, comes only from his letters to me in Otwock when I was on my way to England. It comes also from Betti's letters in which she took great delight in making fun of him, albeit in a loving way. My Uncle Munio, had a theatrical disposition. His writing had always a flowery flourish that expressed so perfectly his personality. He had a special nickname for me, "Hallodri," with which he always addressed me in his letters. It had no meaning, but it made me feel as if he were calling me onto the stage with him.

Betti wrote about my Uncle Munio's theatrical achievements on 8 August 1939 (23):

> And now you do not need to be proud only of Sam, but also of Uncle Munio …. He wrote many, many poems and theater plays [in Yiddish] that were printed … he showed us a newspaper clipping with the following caption: "A Wedding Prank: A Jewish Theater Play, written by M. Schneider, Lwow."

The play had been staged not only in Lwow, but also in Zbaszyn, to a most enthusiastic audience. The lines Betti quoted from the comedy echoed what I had first heard back home: "*Gevalt vos vil mayn nos fin mir, ikh layd dokh fin ir ohn a shir. Gib ikh mit mayn nos a shmek, loift yeder fin mir vek.*" Roughly translated that means: "Help, what does my nose want from me, I suffer from it endlessly. When I sniff everyone runs away from me." Yes, I was proud to have a playwright in my family.

We tried to be as little trouble as we could be, and gratefully stayed with Uncle Munio's family a week or two. But we wanted a place of our own, and managed to find a small "apartment" in town. It was one room for all four of us, no electricity or gas and no kitchen facilities or storage space. No sooner had we settled in, than a telegram came: I was to leave for Otwock to join the Kindertransport. We had forgotten that I was on the list to go to England; we were so preoccupied with turning our empty room into a home for us.

A gift from heaven, the Kindertransport offered me a new life of freedom and untold opportunities that were my mother's greatest hope for her redemption and mine. It stirred great excitement and hectic preparations. My train fare was provided by the local Jewish organization. My dad went to pick up the money and on the way home he stopped to socialize, as was his habit. At one point he reached into his pocket and realized to his horror that his money was gone. Pocket thieves were known to be extremely skilled and ubiquitous in Lwow. What to do? My dad told his troubles to a man he met in the street who, fortunately, was helpful as well as sympathetic. He explained to my dad that most pocket thieves operate as a syndicate and that my dad would have to go to the head of these *ganovim* (thieves), like Fagin in Oliver Twist, and plead his case. So he did. The head of this ring of thieves called his underlings and reproached them for stealing from a Jewish refugee. He ordered the offender to come forward and return the cash to my dad. There was still some honor in this dishonorable profession. My dad got his money back, also the glasses he had not even missed, and the pocket watch, cut off from its chain. I can no longer recall how I came to know about this unbelievable episode.

Time had come again for me to move on. In Hamburg and Zbaszyn our departure was imposed on us by force or by circumstances. This time, however, my leaving my parents and Betti was our own, freely made decision. Yet, it seemed to come too soon. In retrospect, it came in the nick of time. I had barely claimed my corner of our new "home" before learning I had to leave for Warsaw. Shepherded by Mutti, Papa, and Betti, I arrived at Lwow's railroad station. With my suitcase and ticket in hand, I stood on the train platform with Papa, Mutti, and Betti for the few minutes we still had to ourselves. It was time to say good-bye. What did we say to each other? Did we know in our hearts that this would be our last good-bye? Did I give or get a big hug and a kiss? Or was it merely a traditional shaking of hands? How I wish I could have committed this good-bye to my memory. Looking back on it, I believe I had to deny the significance of that moment. I believe I had already learned to steel myself so that the pain of parting would not overwhelm me. I did not see my mother cry, but this moment must have been heartbreaking for her; the last of her boys, the youngest, the one she loved and cared for the most, she had to let go.

I was also very worried about how I would get by on my own, and how I would make myself understood. All I could say was *"ja nie rozumie po polsku, ale ja mowie po niemiecku"* ("I don't understand Polish, but I speak German"). I took some pride in being able to pronounce this phrase properly, but it didn't help me understand when others answered me in Polish.

During all the harrowing time in No-Man's Land and in Zbaszyn, I had been with my parents, safe and protected, or so I felt. Now I started my lonely life. I was not yet 15 years old and had not given any thought to my life away from my parents. All I knew at the time was that there would be a Jewish family in Cardiff, Wales, by the name of Corne, who would take care of me. They would be my foster family. I assumed I would be expected to be a good boy, study and work hard, and be appreciative of my new guardians. It was, of course, not difficult for me to be a good boy or to study hard as that was how I was raised. But accepting my new foster parents as my own proved quite impossible, as time would tell.

The Lwow-Warsaw train rattled and shook through the night. I could not sleep, but I must have dozed off. I arrived in Warsaw the next morning. I was too dazed, fearful and tired during the hours' long train ride to make much sense of what was happening, but I knew I was no longer in any danger of my life. Nor did I shed any tears: I had not quite absorbed the impact of the separation from my parents. A representative from the Refugee Children's Movement picked me up and brought me (together with the other children, who had already been assembled) by bus to Otwock, a small town, some 25 miles southeast of Warsaw. The Kindertransport camp in Otwock was our staging area for our trip to England, by way of Gdynia, Poland's only port city on the Baltic Sea. The weather in this part of Central Poland was sunny, warm and dry, perfect for playing soccer. But we didn't do any of that. I found myself in what looked like a summer camp, but we had few activities. We had English lessons and prepared ourselves for life in England. It did not, however, prepare me for life without my parents around. I could still write to them, get mail from them, and above all, maintain the fantasy that we would be reunited in time.

Propitiously, a renowned rabbi was visiting the Chabad Center in Warsaw at the time, who was taking a side trip to Otwock. That was a serendipitous opportunity for our group of boys to meet him before we sailed off to England. I can't conjure up an image of this rabbi in my mind, nor can I be really sure that it was not the local rebbe who befriended us. If my memory does not fail me, it was possibly Rabbi Schneerson who offered each of us a gift of our choosing as a token of his blessing for our trip and our future. I chose to take the pocket *Tenach*, the Hebrew Bible, condensed to 1388 thin pages, yet only one inch thick (!), bound in a brown leather zippered cover. I have always treasured it. Though I have not used it to study or to pray, it has been a faithful talisman. Its frayed outer edges testify to the travails it shared with me, but the inside pages have remained in prime condition.

There are few other details I can recall from my time in Otwock. I kept my feelings well-repressed, complied with all instructions, and survived in the here and now without much thought to the future.

That left me with little energy ... except for complaining. I must have kvetched throughout my 4-week's stay, judging by the mail I got from my family in Lwow. And that mail, which was my only source of information, came in a steady stream every other day.

The first thing I did in the Kindertransport camp was to write home. My mother's answer came immediately. Since her first card was postmarked <u>26 July 1939</u>, (24) I must have arrived in Otwock a few days earlier. Glad that I had arrived safely, she revealed "you were in a sad mood [when leaving for Warsaw], which was very painful for me, but it is after all for the best." It was not characteristic of my mother to admit her pain, but her trust in a better outcome or her belief in God, was typical of her. I was very sad, but didn't know it. My teary eyes must have betrayed me. Though I know I'm not to blame, in retrospect I nonetheless feel terrible to have caused her such pain.

My mother's next letter of <u>2 August 1939</u> (25) began with her concern and advice regarding my litany of complaints. All kids at camp were to have their hair cut, and I must have protested bitterly. My apparent panic over this prospective shearing was taken so seriously by my mother—and by Betti—that they urged me, as a last resort, to turn to Sam in London for help. (I did. He was very rational about it and assured me that my hair would grow back.) In this instance, and at all subsequent times when no local solutions could be found for problems, my parents and Betti also appealed to Sam, too, as someone with connections, influence, solutions, and the ability to run interference. My mother had great faith in him.

She wrote, "Perhaps it is possible for him to write to prevent it [my haircut]. He should explain that you have been well-cared for at home, and that you are quite particular [about your hair] ...." I never realized I had such an emotional investment in my hair. Although my mother had lots of worries, burdens, and anxieties of her own, she was empathic and hopeful. "This lovely land [meant sarcastically] gives you the cup of bitterness filled to the brim ... but, thank God, help comes nearer every day and every hour." I felt reassured by her fervent hope but not by any belief in help from heaven. My mother's anxious concern for me was my security blanket.

Betti did not lose the opportunity to add a few lines to my mother's letter. She, who knew me well, offered a typically strategic and optimistic piece of advice. She suggested that I move to the end of the haircutting line, so that I could have a better chance to negotiate my haircut. I had complained also about the itching that was driving me crazy. "When I read your card and came to your itching, you can compete with me" she wrote:

> neither should you regard my business as *"shitvesdig"* [as a partnership with you]. I had to laugh, although I felt very sorry for you. Since we have been in Poilen [Yiddish for Poland, meant derogatorily], we want the many different insects (bugs, fleas, etc.) to keep up our connection as they go from me to you and vise versa.

Betti never revealed anything that might have gotten her down. The miseries that beset her or me, she described always in an upbeat or humorous manner, yet she was not insensitive. On the contrary. Sounding very much like an adult at her 17 years, she helped me to deal with my distress. She wanted me to count the days I still had left in Poland, much like the *Omer* that we count from Pesach to Shavuot. Betti usually succeeded in keeping my spirits up.

From mother's postcard of 4 August 1939 (26) I learned that Sam was trying also to get Betti to come to England, and had urged her to write to the "Centos" Committee in Warsaw. Since she was not eligible for the Kindertransport, she would have had to deal with official authorities. In that case, she would have come under the Polish quota according to the English immigration policy at the time. Again my mother exhorted me to keep my money and my books safe and to treat myself to snacks. The frequency of her exhortations suggests that I would not ordinarily have spent money on myself. Always concerned about my health and my welfare, my mother wanted so much to nourish and protect me, but urging me to treat myself to sweets was as much as she could do.

Interestingly, she mentioned that an acquaintance of my father, a certain Herr Bleich, had the same misfortune as my dad: Herr Bleich complained that he, too, had been robbed in Lwow. (Uncle Harry's father, in a letter to Uncle Harry, mentions yet another person who had been robbed in Lwow.) My father was not the only victim of these *ganovim* (thieves), and it strengthened my belief that my father's misadventure was quite credible, after all.

Two days later, on 6 August 1939 (27) my mother wrote a long letter that revealed to me how I had burdened her with my homesickness and misery. I was not yet 15 and had been away from my mother for only 2 weeks. It is with aching guilt that I re-read my mother's letter, and see how I had burdened her with my woes. "When I read your sorrowful, almost despairing letter, I immediately wrote to Sam, enclosed your letter, and urged him not to miss out on any help that might be available." She went on to exhort me "not to take everything so much to heart ... and take some pleasure in whatever you can...think how many of us are thinking of you with love and that they would help you if they could ...."

In the end, compassion must submit to realism. And needy as I was for comfort and reassurance, I had to be confronted with the truth that I was pretty damn fortunate. Uncharacteristically, mother wrote:

> What is your great despair all about? If only I knew, I could perhaps ease it. Many people would be [willing to be] in prison for half a year if they could only know that their frightful life will get better and that they are heading toward a [better] future. When I complain to someone about how I am hurting for you, they laugh at me, because they have bigger problems and would readily exchange places with you. I noticed this materialized on Shabbat; Jewish boys standing in

the street and I looked at them and could have wept, and they even have a home and live with their parents.

Don't let yourself get weak and hung up on bad thoughts because it depresses you and ruins your health. You must maintain a good mood, otherwise life has no value. Do you know the quote "Laugh, Laugh, Bayazzo?"

My mother was referring to a sad-eyed but cheerful clown in Leon Cavallo's opera *I Pagliacci*, implying that I should follow the clown's example and laugh in the face of adversity.

I must have been at camp in Otwock for close to two weeks when I learned from Betti's letter, dated 8 August 1939, (23) that I would not be on the transport leaving 11 August. It is not clear why or how I was expected to leave Otwock for Gdynia on 11 August. It turned out that I was scheduled to leave on the next contingent, 14 days later. Should I not be on the list for the later transport, she said, "Sam would not tolerate another postponement; he will fight for you to leave on the 25th of this month ... let that be a consolation for you." So, Betti would bring to bear the "Big Gun" (Sam) if some problem should arise. It was not necessary; I left on that last day, together with our small group of boys. Sam was very much on top of getting my departure date confirmed. We later learned that ours was the last ship out. How lucky we were!

Sam, who was not known among us as a prompt correspondent, sent an 8-page single-spaced typed letter. The letter, dated 8 August 1939 (28), was actually more like a document or communiqué that he had addressed separately to everyone in my family. It brought us up-to-date on what Sam had been doing for us and for himself, and he made clear that he knew well our situation and what prospects we had for getting help. It marked a turning point in my purgatory and in my outlook. In his address to me, Sam wrote, "Dear Gunther, You can discern from the above lines [his lines to the other members of our family] the matters that concern you [e.g. departure date]." He didn't want to repeat the details. His tone then changed and became warmer and supportive, "Be confident and hang in there bravely for this short time. You have gone through much more, and are after all an up and coming young man. That involves responsibilities. In just 2-3 weeks I'll perhaps be able to shake your hand." I was thrilled to hear that. But from my mother's letters to him, Sam knew of my worries, and understandably admonished me for burdening my mother. With my departure date confirmed, he urged me to change my tone in my letters to my mother:

> I hope you can now sound more confident and with inner calm in your letters to Lwow, so that they do not have to suffer even more than they necessarily have to. Think of the predictable effect every letter you write has on the recipient. You are

otherwise such a thoughtful and considerate boy.

I needed to hear that.

We still had a little over 2 weeks to go before our turn to leave for England. One contingent of boys was ready to ship out on 11th of August. How we envied them! I had let up complaining and focused my anxiety on my departure date. And what if it didn't happen as planned? Uncertainty and mistrust were in the air. Sam came to the rescue with his haranguing the "Centos" Committee in London for a definitive answer, and he indeed obtained an unquestionable assurance that I would be on the next boat out of Gdynia.

The mail from my parents and Betti came faster and faster during the next 2 weeks. The last letter I received in Otwock before I left Poland, dated <u>21 August 1939</u> (29), was filled with the details of their life: the fire down the street, Betti's costly cough medicine, the tailor discoloring my pants that my mother had given him to dye, Lucia's (Uncle Munio's daughter) getting married.... I felt these letters and cards were drawing me still closer to my family just at the time of my imminent departure. I loved Betti's detailed, chatty letter. She charged me with a message for Emil ("Isi") whom she missed terribly.

Betti's message this time was not simply to have me convey her greetings to Isi. Her usual upbeat mood had changed to a serious appeal to Isi that he should not forget her. And not only did she want to be remembered, she pleaded with me to "tell [him] everything"—all that she had experienced during the deportation and since: the dangers and the deterioration of her life; the fears and the fleas. I felt that her *cri de coeur* should be heard by all. I wanted to make it my mission to *tell everybody* what Betti (and my parents) had gone through and how they had suffered. Her outcry still resonates in my ears.

I believed Betti would soon follow me to London, as Sam had promised. Her immigration papers were to be ready in 2-3 weeks, but that was already too late. I also held out hope for a reunion with my parents in London, a faint hope sustained by Sam. I didn't know then that I would never see my parents or Betti again.

Our Kindertransport Group Of Boys In Otwock
Waiting For Our Departure To England, August 1939
(I am the second on the left)

7. From Otwock To Cardiff (1939 – 1941)

The day of my departure from Otwock finally came, on the 25th of August 1939, and it came none too soon. Two days earlier the Nazis and the Soviets had secretly signed the Non-Aggression Pact in which they would divide Poland in half from north to south after they had won and occupied their respective Polish territories. One week later, Poland was mobilizing for war to protect its borders. (Could two demoniacal dictators be trusted to keep the peace after they had despoiled and polluted Poland? Meant to last 10 years, the Non-Aggression Pact was broken by the Nazi invasion of Soviet Russia two years later.)

We boys in Otwock were ready, equipped with all the blessings and good wishes of our families, and with our few belongings. Luggage and labels were checked and rechecked. We boarded the bus to Warsaw and the train to Gdynia, Poland's only outlet to the Baltic Sea, just west of Danzig (Gdansk), the contested seaport. From our all-too-slow moving train we could see Polish soldiers with their military equipment, their trucks and tanks. Some soldiers were stopping men of military age in the street to check their papers. Always eager to hear the news, I heard about the special sessions of the English and French cabinets and of the Nazi-Soviet conspiracy, and I noted in my diary, "These events are signs of a political crisis...bad omens." War fever was in the air and there was no time to be lost. Our train passed undisturbed through Danzig, a usually quiet town that had the whole world in jitters because of the

Nazi threats. Swastika flags could be seen everywhere. (As a semi-autonomous "city-state," Danzig had a predominantly German population that was claimed and later occupied by the Nazis.)

When we arrived at the pier in Gdynia on 25 August 1939, the ship was tied up and waiting. We immediately went on board. We felt as if we had escaped a terrible danger. Indeed, we had. The S/S "Warszawa" was an old Polish passenger ship that seemed to have been only recently put back in service. The ship set sail that same day, and a new chapter began in my life. I kept a log of the days at sea, but it recorded little more than the menus and the boredom of just "being on board," and the constant "looking out at the sea." To my later surprise, I confided no more thoughts in my diary. The ship took the long route to get to London. We skirted the southern coasts of Sweden and Norway to reach the North Sea, rather than taking the shortcut through the Kiel Canal that would have cut our voyage by one day. The captain wisely avoided German waters. He didn't trust the Germans. (Smart move!)

S/S Warszawa

We arrived at the London docks on 29th August 1939, exactly 3 days before Hitler launched his Blitzkrieg against Poland. Hitler's invasion caused England and France, which were bound by a treaty with Poland, to declare war on Germany on the 3rd September 1939. Sam had come to welcome me; he

Photo From My ID Papers 1939

was at the quay and saw me on deck waving to him, and he waved back. I was glad to see him: a familiar face in a strange land. Fourteen months had passed since I last saw him at home on the day we were arrested in Hamburg. My new foster parents, Mr. and Mrs. Corne of Cardiff, who had vouched for me (attesting that I would not become a burden of the state) also met me at the pier.

The arrival of the Kindertransport children from Poland called for a public celebration of sorts. The director of the organization ("Centos") came on board to greet us and another luminary gave a short speech of welcome, which I thought was heartfelt. There was also a reporter from the Jewish press who covered the event. With the ceremonies concluded, I got off the boat, and Sam took the Cornes and me to a fancy Jewish restaurant. In my diary I noted that the dinner was "something I had not even seen in a movie ... the waiters in formal suits with tails were flitting by like the wind, replacing empty bottles with full ones ...." At this feast I did not let my anxiety spoil my appetite, as it has always done, and within the hour I was again offered food at Sam's apartment at 24 Bernard Street. There I met the Silberbergs, Sam's future in-laws. It was all so very exciting, but more than I could take.

The Cornes felt a great sense of urgency because of the ominous war clouds on the horizon and wanted to get me quickly "back home" to Cardiff. No chance to spend a little more time with Sam, to get oriented or to rest a day, let alone go sight-seeing in London. I was too bewildered to register much of a first impression of my benefactors. However, my diary states unequivocally that I thought of Mrs. Corne as "a nice lady," which I would later have to qualify. Mr. Corne looked like a typical Jewish peddler—a characterization he would have readily accepted and would not have offended him. He was a warm and friendly sort, to whom I took an immediate liking. The Cornes had hired a taxi to take us to the railroad station when my stomach rebelled; I had barely climbed inside when I vomited all over the cab. That was my first day in London.

A mere 150 miles west of London and 2½ hours by train, Cardiff is a mid-size city in Wales (though only lately its capital), a seaport in the Bristol Channel. Gloomy, dark grey rain clouds matching my mood greeted our arrival in the late afternoon. It took no time for us to get to 184 Bute Street where the Cornes lived, in the main area of the city's "red light" district. The street led from the city center to the waterfront, which we called "the docks." Mr. Corne had a seamen's outfitter shop that carried virtually everything a seaman might need, from working clothes to condoms. There were other small shops like theirs intermingled with flophouses, taverns, the Salvation Army, and boarded up establishments. It was skid row, populated by drunks, prostitutes, and a few merchants who added some respectability by trying to make an honest living off the seamen who came ashore. The Cornes lived in the back of the store and could see through a small window any customer who would come in. I had a small bedroom upstairs which served me well for my retreats.

And then there was Yenta Corne, a lank, plain girl a few years older than I. She proved to be a friendly, helpful, compassionate pal, and we had a good brother-sister relationship going. Yenta was actually a niece of Mr. or Mrs. Corne who, having no children of their own, adopted her from a member of their extended family. Without detracting from the humanism and generosity of the Cornes, I used to wonder whether they brought me over, in part, to be a companion to their daughter.

In Cardiff I quickly learned to speak English more fluently. The Cornes didn't like me to speak German, but tolerated my lapsing into Yiddish when I could not otherwise make myself understood. We were at war with Germany, and the atrocities of the Nazis had poisoned everything associated with German or Germany. They did not like my German name either, and called me "Gershon." However, they went to great lengths to make me comfortable and welcome and part of their family.

The Cornes In Cardiff, 1939

They took me along whenever they visited other members of their family. How amazed and wide-eyed I was when we were invited to a relative of the Cornes, a theater owner, who had a plush theater room in his own home. I appreciated all the efforts others made to ease my transition to my new life. But I could not feel myself to be a member of their family, because I needed to hold on to my loyalty to my own parents. The Cornes did not want to know anything about my past. But I could not and would not forget my past; I wanted to remember it.

I was an unhappy boy who wouldn't accept easy assurances of a better life in Cardiff. Nor did I count my blessings. My first impression of Mrs. Corne as a nice woman soon vanished, and I came to see her as shrewish and controlling—totally without empathy for me. We didn't fight, but I felt I had to go along with her opinions and decisions, and keep my bitter disappointment to myself. Well, not quite to myself. I know I complained to Sam and, no doubt, to others I had been writing to. I wanted to get away from the Cornes and from Cardiff. I reopened the issue of getting a certificate for Palestine: did I still have the option to go there? Could I make aliyah (immigrate) to Ben Shemen, the Youth Village there? Should I move to London? I knew Sam was in no position to help me the way the Cornes could, and neither were my two sisters in Palestine. I needed to stay and make the best of the situation. And, of course, I had no alternative.

In retrospect, I may have seemed a difficult and ungrateful boy to the Cornes; I was so disappointed and unhappy. They may well have done the best they knew, while I remained closed-off.

Unexpectedly, a solution to my misery and perhaps also to the Cornes' worry, presented itself. I saw a chance for me to get away and to help the war effort. I heard a radio appeal asking all foreigners to volunteer for farm work because most farm hands—like all other British men—had been drafted into the army. We feared a German invasion by sea and Britain was preparing frantically to protect its shores and cities. Although German nationals were treated by Britain as enemy aliens and were subject to arrest and deportation to the Isle of Man in the Irish Sea, I was not detained because I was officially stateless and not a German national. Nonetheless, I was subject to a lot of restrictions. I could not own a bicycle or radio, and had to report to the police station whenever I moved from my home address for any purpose and for any period of time. I still have my Alien Registration booklet, which bears entries recording my every move and every job change within the country.

I responded to the farm appeal, believing that I would meet other young people like myself who were displaced and lonely. I fantasied that I might even meet again some Kindertransport boys I got to know on the way over to England. Of course, there were no refugees on the farm. When and how I got to the Welsh farm I cannot remember, but I still have a clear image of some of my experiences there. The Cornes had better judgment than I, and discouraged me from volunteering for the farm life. They just couldn't imagine me, an undernourished, bespectacled, introverted boy doing farm work! I must have rejected their advice, but was glad to know that I could always come back to them if things didn't work out.

My Alien Registration Booklet

Little did I realize what I had let myself in for. Small in stature with my head in the clouds, I must have been a strange sight to the farmer looking me over. I don't suppose he was impressed with my physique or with my mind, but nonetheless I was another pair of hands. And so I started my stint in the field in 1940, at harvest time. My morning chore was to release the cows in the sheds, about 10 of them, after the farmer had milked them mechanically in their stalls. I made sure that they moved out from their stalls quickly, to make the cleanup job easier for me. I learned who the lead cow was, got her out first, and the other cows would then follow. But there were always a few that were slow to get outside before eliminating their digested cud. They deposited their heap of spinach on the shed floor, which was a treat for the pigs, who in turn, were a big help for me. I didn't think of it then, but what an ecosystem!

My main job, however, was to make hay—in the literal sense—while the sun was shining, and stash it in the barn. The farmer had me rake out the already-cut hay, which was caught in the hedges bordering the field. Although it took a few hours, I did not mind this chore. It was one particular warm and sunny day that I laid down in the field to rest from my labors. After all, I had done my job and there were no further chores assigned to me. What else was there to do? Before long the farmer found me basking in the sun, but my encounter with him was not unpleasant or unexpected. He had decided that I was not suited for farm work, and that was what I thought, too.

So we mutually agreed that I leave after another week's work. When it came to stashing the hay, I found there was more for me to learn. We had no silo or any modern farm equipment, so the bundles of hay had to be lifted from the wagon into the loft of the barn, hoisted up by means of a winch that was pulled by a horse. I walked the horse in a half circle, not knowing that the horse sidesteps as he turns, and that I had better do the same. I learned my lesson when I felt the horse's left leg on my right foot. Fortunately the ground was soft and my bones were not broken. And that wasn't all.

I also learned something during the second week about tending farm animals that went beyond feeding them, or grooming the horse, and shearing the sheep. The farmer had me watch how he castrated the little squeaking piglets, and he didn't miss the opportunity to warn me jokingly to look out lest that happen to me. I laughed politely, but was not amused. And then there was the primal scene of the bovine sort. The cow had to be corralled and the mounting bull's penis had to be hand-guided to inseminate her. That was a scene to remember for a sensitive and innocent, virginal boy.

I was glad to get back to Cardiff. I returned "home" to the Cornes, quite contrite and more respectful of them. Although still in the existential fog in which I had left them two weeks earlier, I reconciled myself to staying with my foster family for the duration. I had written off my daydreams of going to Palestine, which I believed would one day be the State of Israel. However, I still had papers pending for immigrating to the States, and this prospect gave me hope for an eventual normal life. I got many letters of support, compassion, and advice from Sam and Simon. They really came through for me when I needed them.

Settled into my life with the Cornes, I was drawn into service "watching the shop." I called my "uncle" or "aunt" from "the back" when a customer would come in, and generally tried to help out. I did not wait on customers, or handle cash, but Mr. Corne trusted me to prepare checks for charities. He never allowed a single request for a donation to go unanswered. His quiet, unheralded generosity was not lost on me, it became my ideal, but I cannot claim to have lived up to it. While I liked being in the store and enjoyed the paper work, I had the chance to do something far more exciting with Mr. Corne. To make sure that our customers (mostly sailors) would not spend all their money elsewhere on our street before coming to our store, Mr. Corne used to take samples of all his wares, bundle them up, go to the pier and board every ship that came to call. When a ship was not tied to the pier, but was anchored in the harbor, he took a small boat and climbed up the Jacob's ladder (the rope ladder on the side of the ship), spread out his "goods" in the crew's mess hall, and "took orders." And I went with him. I had my bundle to carry, but Mr. Corne did all the bargaining and negotiating. He could both count, and name his merchandise, in several languages—which was all he needed to bargain in Chinese, French, or Italian. (We had no ships from China, but many ships had Chinese crews.)

At some point, probably soon after my return from the farm, Mrs. Corne enrolled me in the 8th grade of the local elementary school, although I was already a year older than my classmates. I was "to learn the language." At the end of the semester, the principal decided that I had sufficiently mastered the language, and there was nothing more for me to gain at his school. Why didn't Mrs. Corne arrange to have me go on to high school? It was not for me to argue or protest. I don't recall that my going on to high school was a matter of discussion. It probably was not considered necessary for me. But I decided that I could at least go to night school. Twice a week I walked at night for a half hour through the darkened streets of Cardiff to get to school. The only courses available to me were Commercial Law (without a high school diploma!) and shorthand (Pittman's), where I won a shorthand dictionary as a prize. I thought I might one day work in an office that could lead some day, somehow, to what I believed was an exalted business position like Sam had back in Hamburg. I then decided to educate myself and bought an encyclopedia for self-study, a thick book with lessons in several high school subjects, but I didn't get very far. I couldn't master the hard sciences on my own and no help was available.

With my continued education sidelined, Mrs. Corne had me look for a job. I thought she wanted me to contribute to my upkeep, since I had to pay for my shoe repairs and various other incidental expenses out of the pocket money she gave me. In retrospect, Mrs. Corne meant well; she wanted to help me grow up as a self-supporting young man. She searched the newspaper's help wanted section and found an opening at a delicatessen for an errand boy. Dutifully I applied, but was repulsed by my first look at this establishment. It was filthy inside and rats were running around. I didn't want to work there for anything. When the owner told me he could not bring himself to have a nice Jewish lad do such dirty work for him, I silently agreed and was relieved to be turned down for the job. Mrs. Corne, on the other hand, was incensed that a Jewish employer would turn down a Jewish boy, and a refugee to boot, with such a flimsy excuse, depriving him of a small livelihood. My search for employment continued. I next applied at a shoe store that was a branch of a chain, called "Halewood," at the far end of Bute Street. The store manager, Mr. J. Mitchell, was a lovely, gentle, kind, elderly Scottish man; a father figure to whom I could readily relate. Although my officially recorded status was that of an errand boy, he promoted me right away to sales assistant. He took a personal interest in me and taught me all about the trade: making, selling, and repairing shoes. More importantly, we had daily discussions about philosophy and religion. He was keenly interested in my background, and he invited me one day to dinner at his home. There was also a girl working in the store, about my own age (I was 16 at the time), who waited on women customers and handled the stock. She was exotic, possibly Eurasian or of mixed ethnic background, very vivacious and fun loving. We chased each other around the stacks of shoeboxes in the attic of the store. It was all so innocent.

When Mr. Mitchell was absent from the store, he left me in charge. He groomed me for promotion, but much to his regret could not offer me a better position at Halewood. I had no future in his firm, he told me. So he had me apply for a better job at a competitor and told me what to say should I be asked why I could come in the middle of the workday for an interview. But I did not follow up; I had set my sights on going to London. I worked for Mr. Mitchell until the day I left Cardiff, and on my last day he gave me the Oxford Pocket Dictionary as a parting gift, which I still have and cherish. I shall never forget him. He had a special way of writing his initial "J," which I have unconsciously adopted in my own writing style. And I have often dreamt of him.

Halewood Shoe Store, Cardiff, 1940
(Mr. Mitchell at entrance)

While all was quiet on the Western Front, a time that was aptly named the "Phony War," Hitler's diabolical war in Poland was deadly and devastating. In just 4 weeks Warsaw fell to the Nazis and their armed forces occupied Poland up to the border, as Hitler had previously arranged in a secret pact with the Soviets. Lwow was a few miles within the Soviet side. At that point, all mail, all news from Lwow stopped. There was no word of any kind from my parents or Betti. I was very worried about them and shared my anxieties with Sam. He had no more luck than I trying to find out what happened to our parents. He made inquiries at the Soviet embassy in London, but to no avail. We just had to wait it out until the gun smoke cleared.

For over three months no mail went to or from Soviet occupied Eastern Poland. It was not until 28

January 1940 (30) that I again heard from my parents, who were as worried about me as I was about them. "Should you get this card," my mother wrote, "[know that] we are in good health...only may God bring peace." Delighted and thankful for the card I had sent her, my mother plaintively noted that it had taken a full two months to get there. What fears, privations, and persecutions they must have endured during these several months, yet not a word about them, only concerns about us in Britain, expressions of hope, and good wishes for all of us. From January 1940 to shortly before the German forces stormed across the border into Soviet Russia in June 1941, I was in constant contact with my parents in Lwow, sending and receiving postcards often several times a week.

My mother had tried to keep up her hope of getting out alive; at least she kept her faith in God. She assured me that they had food to eat, but no income to sustain them. So she sold whatever of her belongings would bring some money to keep them afloat. Her postcard of 18 February 1941 (31) heartbreakingly revealed how impoverished their life had become:

> Dear child, my big boy. I answer every postcard of yours. Does it get there? Who knows, perhaps we will soon not be able to write at all, then we will trust God and wait. Things were terrible in London, and who knows what may yet come .... We are in good health and hope to endure .... Everything in the crates has been sold.

> Even the crates have been used up [for firewood?].

One month later, I heard from my mother for the last time.

Britain was getting ready for an invasion by the Nazis, and for the air attacks that were sure to come. All windows were securely taped so they would not shatter into shards of glass in an explosion. Total blackout was enforced and torches (flashlights) papered over so that only a slit of light would shine. Radios were set for newscasts that came every hour. Air raid shelters were built on many streets. Ours looked like a Quonset hut and was just across the street from us. Many busy intersections sprouted overnight concrete machine gun nests that looked like little silos with open slots in their walls. Air raid sirens blared their screaming sounds, and searchlights swept the black sky at night.

In 1940-41 Cardiff's defenses were put to the test. Hitler meant to intimidate the British population and sent his bombers to blast us into submission. But Hitler underestimated Churchill and the British people. Hitler boasted he would wring England's neck like that of a chicken. "Some chicken, some neck!" was Churchill's famous reply to Hitler. News of this mass bombing of London went, of course, around the world. My parents read the papers and were very worried. Wary of the censor, my mother let me know in one short Yiddish sentence, written upside down in a corner of the postcard, on <u>18 October 1940</u>, (32) that the news was too upsetting. "To read in the papers what is going on in London one can go crazy."

While London was the main target of Hitler's blitzkrieg, Cardiff got its share. Cardiff was a major port for the export of Welsh coal, still the major fuel for Western industries, a fact not lost to the German Luftwaffe in their air attacks. We were at the receiving end of intermittent bombing attacks with the heaviest of raids occurring on 2 January 1941, which entered the records as the "Cardiff Blitz." Every night when the alarm sounded I grabbed the survival kit I kept next to my bed, and rushed over with the Cornes to the shelter across the street. The shelter was a cement Quonset hut set on the pedestrian pavement. Inside, it had long wooden benches on both sides of the wall, but no light or heat. That is where I spent the night, on the bench, half asleep until the "all clear" sounded several hours later. We heard bombs exploding and fragments hitting our shelter, and we huddled but did not cower. Then back to our house and back to bed. But as we emerged from our shelter, we saw buildings burning that lit up the sky, and emergency vehicles rushing hither and yon with sirens blaring. Our house was not hit, but some buildings on our street were demolished.

Yenta, my foster sister, was undaunted by these attacks on Cardiff. She liked to go to the movies, sometimes twice a week, and I went with her. Coming home from the theater one evening, we found ourselves in the middle of an air raid. (Movies kept going when the sirens sounded.) We ran from one house to another, taking momentary shelter in the doorways, looking up in the sky to see if any bombs were falling. Fortunately we made it back safely.

The war outside was nothing to laugh at, but we had fun indoors. The Cornes had a young woman from Jamaica who cleaned the house and helped out in the store when needed. She didn't take herself or her life seriously. She loved to play. During breaks in her work, she would keep Yenta and me company and entertain us with stories or get into what I thought was horseplay with me. She would throw me onto the sofa and herself on top of me. She sure got her kicks out of trying to seduce me, but Yenta's presence served to keep her play within bounds.

One day some money was missing from the store. Who could have taken it? Certainly not anyone in the family, and not our trusted help. Oddly, I thought that it somehow must have been me, although I could not imagine how I could possibly have done such a thing. Perhaps I was temporarily dissociated or was sleepwalking, unaware of my own actions? That Kafkaesque sense of guilt plagued me day and night. We finally found out that our Jamaican woman had done the foul deed. She was clearly not as trustworthy as we had assumed. She was fired, but it took me a long while to get over it, although no one had ever openly accused me.

Sam knew well how badly I felt about my life in Cardiff, but there was nothing much he could do from London other than to write encouraging letters. His marriage to his first wife, Edith, had come to an end, and so had his export business. The war at sea had made overseas shipping on which Sam's export business depended, impossible. He was now reduced to making a living driving a truck. For me to move to London and be near him was not an option, because he was not in the position to help me in any way. However, out of his sense of responsibility for his little brother, who had burdened him so often about his loneliness, Sam appealed to a social agency for help for me. Sam must have thought that my getting to know some friendly people in Cardiff, whom I could visit, might allay my lonely feelings. Well, I got a letter from the agency, giving me the name and address of a volunteer family who had invited me for Sunday tea. That was not what I had been thinking of, or what I had hoped Sam would do. These well-intentioned people were strangers to me, and were not Jewish. How could I possibly feel comfortable with them, I thought. They were an older couple without children, living in one of those row houses that stretched endlessly along the road, which you would see when traveling through the mining towns of South Wales. I felt I could not back out of it, and I went to see these good people, but it took something out of me. I tried my best to make them feel they were doing me a great service by opening their home to me for an afternoon. But I didn't feel good about that and I never went back.

Events in the year 1941 I will never forget. I was still living with the Cornes in Cardiff, although I was preparing for my move to London later that year, when Hitler broke the non-aggression pact with Stalin on 22 June 1941 and sent his invincible army east across the Soviet frontier. Lwow, where my parents and Betti lived, was the first to fall to the Nazi army. The attack was unexpected and came quickly. The German troops had their *einsatzgruppen* (special SS detachments) whose mission was to render the newly-occupied areas

Judenrein. The "Final Solution" had begun. Some years later, when the Nazi atrocities were documented and published, I learned that most of Lwow's Jews had been gassed at the Belzec extermination camp. A large number also were killed in their homes and in the streets. I never learned my family's precise fate.

Sam had urged my parents earlier to move farther east, but that was not possible for them. They had no resources or person to turn to for such a move. Where in the vast Soviet hinterland could they go, and how would they get there? We had hoped for the best, but feared the worst. The last piece of mail I received from Lwow is a postcard, dated <u>14 March 1941</u> (33), which held no hint of the doom that came three months later. My mother wrote:

> My most beloved Guntherl! I'm sitting and writing to all my children who recently wrote to me. From you, child of my heart, I have the most mail. Our mail carrier is happy every time he comes to us, because he always gets something for his trouble.... From 13 September until today times have been tough, and all I want to know is about your health, because there is no shortage of woes.... Perhaps Betti will soon find a job.... May God grant us a peaceful summer, not like the previous one which we have not yet forgotten. We are in good health. Only peace has to come like a miracle.

Three more months passed without mail or news from Lwow. What could have happened? I firmly believe it simply was not possible for my mother to write during that time; the family's position must have been deteriorating and their resources, undoubtedly, had run out. If my mother had paper and pen, the money for the postage, the strength and the opportunity, I am convinced she would have written.

Many of my letters and cards to Lwow were returned "undeliverable." I saved those, too. They document my desperate, but futile effort to get a sign of life from my family.

Returned Letters

I wrote to the Red Cross and other relief organizations for news about my family over there, but they could not help. I appealed to the Chief Rabbi of Sweden, but never got an answer. I never thought that my parents could have survived; yet I could not openly mourn my loss. It was only in my dreams that I allowed myself to cry, although the bed pillows bore no evidence for it. I longed for many years to have an understanding rabbi help me release my tears and allow me to scream, but I also struggled to keep that longing under control. As an adult many years later, when I felt less vulnerable, I no longer idealized rabbis as comforters. I came to see them simply as men with problems of their own.

Sam was also busy trying to trace the whereabouts of our parents, but with no more luck. Nonetheless, in Sam's letters to me he repeatedly asked whether I had any response to my enquiries about our parents, and he still expressed the hope that they may have escaped to the interior of Soviet Russia, as he had urged them to do. Even had they succeeded, Sam reasoned, no news could be expected for a long time. I was not yet 17 and still in Cardiff when we anxiously exchanged letters about where we had turned for information and what results we had obtained. At the end of our months of research, I resigned myself to the disappearance of my remaining family ... an end without a closure. Sam, too, gave up hope. I think the powerful evidence of the Holocaust in reports from the killing fields, the return of my letters, and the discouraging answers to my pleas for news from agencies convinced me of the inexorable loss of my parents and Betti.

And where was God? Did I really believe at that time in a God who ordered or intervened in the lives of people? I doubt whether I ever did, although my family and my religious education would have me believe it. My cultural identity as a Jew remained firm, though not my faith. How could I cry out to God for such atrocities if I did not believe in Him? I could not resolve the issue. Nor did I allow myself to dwell on it. I rationalized my refusal to mourn openly on the grounds that I do not know the date when my parents and Betti were murdered. But I suspect that it was also my silent, passive protest to God (whom I did not believe in), an irrational protest that I yielded only decades later. I never appealed to God for any comfort or favors, except for the survival of Mutti, Papa, and Betti. And this was my only prayer, unspoken, left on my lips.

Yet there were signs that I had merely repressed my pain. Along with my avoidance of saying Kaddish, I was tightlipped when it came to the Yizkor prayer (in memory of deceased family members) on special holy days. Only attending services in traditional synagogues offered me moments of nostalgic condolence. Many years later when the Holocaust entered the consciousness of the popular culture, in film and in books, I realized my vulnerability, and was very selective in my choice of entertainment.

In retrospect I see I had clearly been in denial because I had maintained hope without my having been aware of it. Or perhaps it was only an impossible dream that emerged five years after I had consciously accepted the irreversible reality of the loss and was settled safely in Chicago: I found myself strangely intrigued by lower middle-class housing that I was passing by. I fantasied how I might rent and rehabilitate such a place for my parents and Betti, a fantasy based on wishful thinking. There was still that yearning in me as a young adult to see them in my new world and to care for them. Why this compelling preoccupation? Was it to redeem my guilt over having survived them?

8. From Cardiff To London (1941 – 1946)

In the fall of 1941 I was 17 and saw no future for me in Cardiff. I told the Cornes about my plans to move to London. They were understanding and wished me well, though they were quite willing to have me stay. Saying goodbye to Mr. and Mrs. Corne and to Yenta was not painful for me. I had not allowed myself to relate to their family as my own. I imagine I said goodbye to them quickly and unemotionally, but here again my memory fails me. I kept in touch with them for a time after I left for London and also after I arrived in Chicago. Over the years I corresponded periodically with Yenta, but those exchanges became more sporadic as the years went by, and they eventually ended after her parents died.

Before I left Cardiff, the war in England had a brief respite, and I had no reason to fear resettling in London. The previous year, the German Luftwaffe had already exhausted its first onslaught on London. England had won the historic Battle of Britain, and the Royal Air Force again ruled the skies. When I arrived in London, the barrage balloons were still dotting the sky, but they were no longer necessary; they had prevented the Luftwaffe from flying low over London, which could have made their bombing more accurate. However, more bombing was still to come from missiles and rockets fired from across the English Channel.

Sam had indicated that he could arrange for me to live in London, and I was ready to start a new chapter in my life. I hoped to live with Sam, continue my education, and plan for an eventual career there. Surely in London I would find opportunities I didn't have in Cardiff. I also anticipated that moving to London would free me from my loyalty conflict with the Cornes. And being close to Sam would make me feel at home. Or so I thought.

As it turned out, I did not get to stay with Sam, and that was a big disappointment. He had a small apartment that could not comfortably accommodate me. Nor did he have the resources to help me financially. So he arranged for me to stay with a nice Jewish family he knew. This family, whose name I can no longer recall, lived in Hendon, in the Northern part of London, which was a very pleasant residential middle class area. I stayed in a room in the family's apartment, but did not join the family at mealtimes. I was very preoccupied with furthering my education and getting a job, and I tended to isolate myself, but not always successfully. The family had a daughter, about my age, who came to my room in the evening, which I naively thought was to "shoot the breeze." I liked her. She was pretty and talkative, and she liked to sit on my bed chatting with me. While I enjoyed her company, my hormones were raging, and it was hard for me to control my youthful impulses. Although at the time it might have been an exercise in good judgment, later in life I came to view such missed opportunities in a different light.

My second disappointment was Sam's separation from his wife, Edith. (His marriage to her was very short lived.) I was terribly fond of Edith, a very pretty, slender brunette whom I met in Hamburg when she was Sam's girlfriend and I was Sam's "little brother." Her warmth and liveliness, which I found so disarmingly attractive, were a perfect counterpoint to Sam's more formal personality. She and her mother got out of Germany before the war; they immigrated to England, and settled in London. Shortly thereafter Sam and Edith got married, but they didn't stay married for long. I may have taken my cue from their reaction to their seemingly amicable divorce, because neither Sam nor Edith appeared to be depressed about it. I suspect it was a greater loss for Sam than he was able to show or admit. I missed Edith. She had always been affectionate toward me. After her divorce she kept in touch with me for several months.

Sam was a proud, self-possessed man, even a little vain. He was very handsome, but it was not only his appearance that was important to him; he needed to maintain a certain status. Before the war, when he made business trips to London from Hamburg, he came as a representative for his employer, HAPAG. For reasons unknown to me, he did not get, or take, a position in London with his former firm after his arrival in England. He instead started a small export business of his own. He didn't have much luck. Soon after the war started, German U-Boats made British overseas shipping very hazardous, and Sam's business simply sank—like so many ships. From that time on Sam's life took a downturn from which he never quite recovered.

This was a period in Sam's life when he took different jobs about which he would not tell me anything. Looking back, I find it strange that I knew so little about his work; I was, after all, also in

London and closer to him than before. I do know that Sam drove a truck for a time, and that it must have been humiliating for him to talk about it. He also worked for the British government in some secret capacity and, understandably, "kept mum." At some point Sam got a draft notice from the Free Polish government in London. He was still a Polish national, but he had the option to refuse service in the Free Polish forces if he enlisted instead in the British army. He did sign up, and was stationed in southern England. When he had furlough he would go on short trips in the country with some army buddy. But he would always write to me, whether he was in camp on duty, or off on some jaunt.

Although I got together with Sam whenever we could, I remember spending much of my time working and studying. I could not go to high school during the day because I had a job, and all evening classes had been cancelled. However, classes were held on weekends, and I enrolled in several courses to prepare for the matriculation examination that I would need to get into college. Naturally I made my study plan as easy on myself as I could. I took English and Math (required), French and Geography (electives). For my third elective I chose German, for which I did not have to study. Years later I took the exams in two sessions and passed, which qualified me to enter the University of London. But I did not remain long enough in London to go to college.

During those years of study I also had to support myself. I went back to selling shoes, which was the only real work experience I had. I got a job as a salesman in a Dolcis shoe store, the biggest and perhaps the best shoe chain in London. The store was located on High Street in Acton, the west side of London. I now dealt with a better class of customers and learned the finer points of the trade. In the modern age, fashion has always trumped fit in the case of ladies shoes, and when I worked at Dolcis, narrow shoes were the fashion in London. For women who wanted the latest style, I needed to find a way to widen these fashionable but narrow shoes while maintaining their shape. I would disappear with the shoes to the back of the store, yank the inside vamp on a broomstick to push the leather out, and return triumphantly telling my customer that I had used the "electric stretcher" so that the shoes would now be sure to fit. I was on commission. I learned to push shoe polish and various accessories that my customers hadn't come to buy, to help fatten my paycheck. The store manager, Mr. Chatterton, an ugly but archetypical Englishman, called me "Glover," which was supposed to be some kind of abbreviation of my long, unpronounceable name (Zloczower). He liked my work and my interest in arranging window displays, but he was no Mr. Mitchell. Mr. Chatterton was a lascivious man who used to grope the shapely sales girls in the back of the store. The seamen on Bute Street in Cardiff had a little more integrity. They paid for their pleasure. With career opportunities limited at the time, I continued as a shoe salesman at Dolcis until the fall of 1943.

Meanwhile in July 1942 I looked for another place to live. I don't recall how I found the Crummenerls, but that was a stroke of luck. They had a neat little house in a beautiful part of London, called Hampstead Garden Suburb, and I rented a room from them. The Crummenerls were glad to have me live with them and, since they had no children of their own, they treated me like a son. They, too, had emigrated from Germany because Mrs. Crummenerl was Jewish while Mr. Crummenerl was not. He left Germany with his wife because he would not abandon her. According to the Nuremberg laws, a non-Jewish husband or wife could save him/herself only by divorcing the Jewish spouse. I admired Mr. Crummenerl for his liberalism and integrity and we had many good political and philosophical talks. It was as if I had found another Mr. Mitchell. It was at that time and place that I developed my idea of how I wanted to live. I wanted a house in a garden suburb: modest, comfortable, and removed from the hustle and bustle of city life, an idyllic retreat. (And, years later in America, I found it.)

Me with the Crummenerls
London, 1941

Hampstead Garden Suburb,
London

Life in London in 1942 was far from normal; air raids still sounded at night, food and clothing were strictly rationed, and above all we heard daily the admonition, "don't you know there's a war on?" (and for travelers, the reproach, "is your trip really necessary?"). The Crummenerls knew how to adapt to the nightly danger. They had a steel shelter in their living room, which we crawled into when the alert sounded. Its base and its top were steel plates, and the sides were made of steel mesh. It was the size of a king size bed and an attractive cover converted it into a table by day.

I had volunteered to be an air raid warden, and with my steel helmet, armband, and whistle, my job was to watch out for incendiary bombs and give the alarm. One night, I was stationed on the roof of a furniture store—a little too risky for me to be so high up and exposed. I decided that I could still perform my watch from inside the building. But I was desperately tired. Mattresses were piled high everywhere, and were most inviting. Unable to resist the temptation, I laid myself down on a stack of mattresses, and promptly fell asleep. Fortunately there was no fire and I did not get into any trouble.

I did not have much of a social life during my London years. Between working every day and taking classes on the weekend, I had little opportunity to find friends. But I did not feel lonely. I passed the time with hobbies I enjoyed. Notwithstanding the fact that owning a radio was still *verboten* for me (because I was still an enemy alien), I had one and would often listen to classical music. To this day that has remained one of my favorite pastimes.

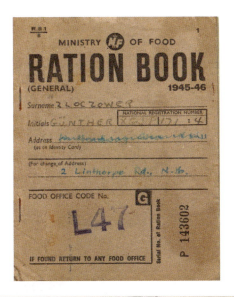

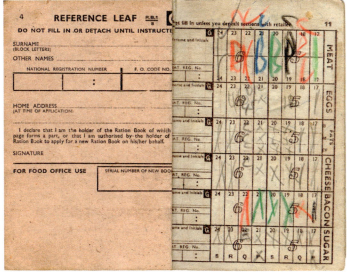

My Ration Book

Another hobby of mine was taking pictures of any pretty scene I could find in the neighborhood, using an old folding camera Sam had given me. I experimented for a time with aperture and shutter speed and composition, and I pursued my photography interest for a time after my arrival in Chicago.

At the end of summer 1943 I decided to make a job change that I thought had prospects for my future. Selling shoes was not a career for me. I had no idea or any guidance as to what I should do and I had no one to guide me. Perhaps I should learn to be a chemist, I wondered. I went to several laboratories that I had picked out from the telephone directory and asked them whether they needed any help. I said I was interested in the field and promised to study chemistry, but all I had to offer was my willingness to learn and work hard. Not surprisingly, that was not quite enough, so nothing became of that. I then turned to Sam, who suggested I give office work a try, and I followed his advice.

I found a job in the office of "Elmat," a small wholesaler of cosmetics and beauty accessories in London. The company purchased half-finished items from a manufacturer and assembled them into finished products. Five people worked on the assembly in the back of what once was an apartment. I had a desk in what could only euphemistically be called the "front office." I kept the books, maintained the correspondence, and answered the telephone. I well remember one day, when I was busy making ledger entries and simultaneously answered the telephone, my boss came by and told me to write a letter. (He would tell me only the gist of the letter and I had to compose it; I never practiced my short hand.) "I'm sorry," I said, "I can't do three things at once." "Then I will teach you how," was his answer. He was a Jewish refugee from Czechoslovakia, quite a taskmaster, and pragmatic. I didn't know how to type properly, but I learned to peck away rapidly with my two fingers (I still do) and, after I had gained some confidence and skill, I approached my boss and asked him for a raise. He promised to raise my salary when I could type as well as his wife! Of course, I never saw his wife or knew how well she typed. Although I was not exactly happy with my job, I decided to stay and work myself into the business to the point where I might become indispensible. Oh, the foolish ideas of my youth; I should have known better.

Only three months later in December 1943, a government official from the Ministry of Labor came to our office looking for manpower to do war work. With the growing shortage of labor in England, the government resorted to recruiting workers from nonessential industries and businesses. The official told my boss that one of his workers must go. Last hired, first fired. I had to go. That put an end to my career plans for the duration of the war. I had hoped to lead a normal, productive life, but this hope was pre-empted by my service to the English war effort.

My first "war assignment" was to report to a factory for training. It was the end of 1943 and I was 19 years old. I had worked on a farm, in shoe stores, and in an office, but I had never pictured myself working in a factory. But there I was, in a hangar-like machine shop, learning to operate a center lathe. It was a case of man against machine, and I won the fight. I was as diligent learning the craft as I was studying French conjugations. And I drew free hand the lathe that I had been working on, a small achievement that gave me some pleasure. However, the worst part of the job was getting to work and tolerating the three rotating shifts, from 6 a.m. to 2 p.m., from 2 p.m. to 10 p.m., and from 10 p.m. to 6 a.m. I could not cope with that. When most people were still asleep, I had to get ready to go to work. And when others were done with their day, late in the evening, I had to start my shift. I never knew whether I was coming or going. This crazy schedule took a toll on me and I came up with some excuse to quit.

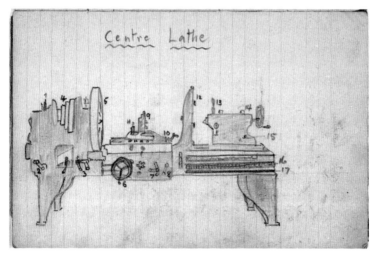

My Centre Lathe Drawing

My next job three months later was no walk in the park, either. The U. S. Army Officers Mess had officially requested kitchen help for their cafeteria, and the Ministry of Labor decided that I was just the man for the job. The Mess served thousands of meals around the clock, but my job was not to prepare any food, cook it, or serve it. My job was to scrape the dirty food trays and stack them in a gargantuan dishwasher—fast and nonstop. It was sordid in that kitchen, steamy and stifling. The kitchen help I worked with were low-life, possibly ex-convicts for all I knew, judging by their coarse language and crude sense of humor. I had jumped from the frying pan into the fire. My vocational life had reached a low point, but there was one compensation: I had good American food to eat and plenty of it. Never mind that most of it came from cans, it still was gourmet compared to what I could obtain with my ration stamps.

Two weeks in that kitchen was all I could stand. Somehow I managed to persuade the supply sergeant, Sgt. Boland, who hailed from California, to get me transferred out of the kitchen to his supply office. After all, I had clerical work experience! I now had an office job, I worked with G.I.s, and I ate their food. Nothing could have been better. I set about organizing the office like Sgt. Boland had never seen before, and he appreciated my work. At breakfast (the first thing at work) he taught me to put salt on my grapefruit (!) like he did, and I was only too happy to follow his example. He was a friendly boss, totally informal, and not worn down by the war, all in sharp contrast to my previous experience at "Elmat" and with my later work for the railroad.

I was 19 and working in the supply office of the U. S. Army Officers' Mess when General Eisenhower came over the public address system addressing the troops. The combined English and American armies were crossing the English Channel. It was D-Day, June 6, 1944, and the tone of Ike's message clearly conveyed the historical significance of the moment with his typical modesty and belief in heavenly as well as earthly powers. Everyone in the cafeteria seemed transfixed and stood at attention. We were glued to the broadcast, and here I was among the Americans, sharing this historical moment! Would my luck hold? With the war raging on the European continent, I wanted to join up, too. However, Sam was dead set against it and, I must admit, I was never really adventurous or intrepid.

While in the British army, Sam kept in close touch with me. When I had a brief stay in a local hospital for a medical procedure, Sam sent me a letter on <u>26 August 1942</u> (34), in which he addressed me cheerfully as "Old Boy," and went on to write in an intimate mood. "You must be quite an Apollo and, no doubt, you will have to be doubly careful about those girls, who can't [help] but go after any nice looking face.... I'm becoming quite a bit of a hermit, but we shall make good for all of that in our holidays." He seemed to feel lonely, and he promised to take me to see the film "Mrs. Miniver" when we would next get together, because that was, as he saw it, the only current, interesting movie to see in all of London. My long cherished wish to be with Sam in London evidently found an echo in his life, and from that time on my hope was fulfilled. I finally felt close to him. Was that my unemotional, formal, distant brother? I had never given him credit for his unexpressed brotherly feelings.

When the allied armies began to sweep across the Continent, the Allied Command needed men who spoke European languages, offering immediate citizenship to any alien who volunteered for the Office of Strategic Services, the forerunner of the C.I.A. I wanted to sign up, but a lot of refugees had the same idea I did. The G.I.s were known (by the British) as "overpaid, overfed, and oversexed." Any wonder I was ready to take the risk of joining? When I applied, however, all openings were filled. But I did not give up hope of serving in the American forces. After all, I was of draft age, and still had the option of going to the U.S. after the war. (I did volunteer after my arrival in the U.S.) I was really happy with my work and with my life during that time in London, but it was too good to last.

It wasn't long before the Ministry of Labor found something more important for me to do than to work for the Americans. Sgt. Boland, who didn't want to lose me, objected and appealed on my behalf, but to no avail. I had to go to work for the railroad; specifically, for the cartage office of the L.M.S. (London, Midlands, and Scottish) Railroad. That office was literally a hole in the wall, located inside a berm under a viaduct, drab and dingy. Draymen (these were the horse cart drivers) came in and out. Their job was to deliver packages that had been shipped by the railroad. They looked like the scarecrow in the Wizard of Oz, wearing tattered attire covered in the hay that they used to feed their horses. I could not understand their Cockney accent, nor could I relate to them. I felt like Charles Dickens' David Copperfield in the ink factory, tossed into a strange and fearful world in which I had to survive. The "office" consisted of long wooden counters that were our desks, with high bar stools for us to sit on. And there were files and files.... My job was to process claims for undelivered packages. I had to learn a new work rule: when someone claimed he did not receive a shipment, I was told to leave the papers in the in-box for a few days or a week. The goods would eventually show up and that would save much time and trouble. I had reached another low in my work life but, again, with one compensation. Because I was now working for the railroad I was entitled to free train tickets every so often.

After three months in the bleak office at Broad Street Station, good fortune smiled on me once again. The Ministry of Labor transferred me to another L.M.S. branch office in Brompton-Fulham in the northeast of London. Rescued from the hay-strewn hole in the wall, I was sent to work with decent people in a decent railroad office. One of my co-workers was a small middle-aged man with sparse blond hair, a ruddy face, and slightly stooped shoulders, by the name of Chipchase. I was so intrigued by his illustrative name that I went to a library to look it up in a dictionary of names. He was amazed when I told him the origin and meaning of his name, which he had never known. It referred, of course, to the aristocratic sport of the foxhunt.

Mr. Chipchase, who readily engaged me in philosophical and political discussions, was a Communist who spouted the typical Communist dogma. Though opinionated, he wasn't closed-minded, and I had no difficulty arguing my liberal democratic points of view. During lunchtime I sought the quiet, restful atmosphere of the nearby cemetery for eating my sandwich and giving my imagination free reign.

Me With The Staff At Brompton-Fulham
(Mr. Chipchase in the middle, back row)
London, 1943

I used my first free railroad ticket to visit Cambridge one weekend. Having enrolled earlier in the British Hostel Association, I could afford to stay overnight at the youth hostel there. I had chosen to go to Cambridge in part because it was only a short trip, but mostly because I wanted to explore the university campus to see what it looked and felt like—although I had no illusions about studying there. At the hostel I met a guy who befriended me, and the two of us set out to explore the area. He was quite knowledgeable about the history of Cambridge and had a guidebook with him. I was terribly impressed when we went to a medieval church and he rolled up the runner in the center aisle to reveal a hidden bronze plaque, inscribed with the name of some famous English churchman who was buried there. That experience sparked my interest in English history.

With another freebie from the L.M.S., I went to Edinburgh just to check out this historic town. I got around by streetcar never knowing exactly where I was going. On one of my rides through town, a Scottish woman who saw that I was a tourist and thought I might be lost, offered to help me. This was perhaps no remarkable event, except that I was struck by her kindness. I decided that I would return one day to revisit this friendly land, and I did many years later.

On another trip, courtesy of the L.M.S., I went to the Lake District. I hiked from one youth hostel to the next, drinking in the beauty and romance of the gentle hills and cool lakes that had inspired some of England's greatest poets. My illustrated album of that memorable vacation records that it rained, which was rather typical for the area. But the rain didn't dampen my enthusiasm. I still can recall some lines from Robert Southey's poem about the wondrous waterfall I saw at Lodore in Cumbria, England:

>How does the water
>Come down at Lodore?"
>My little boy asked me ...
>
> * * *
>
>Rising and leaping,
>Sinking and creeping,
>Swelling and sweeping ...

* * *

> All at once and all o'er,
> And this way the water
> Comes down at Lodore.

What a beautiful verbal rendering of nature's sound.

And that brings me to 1944 another eventful year in England. The Allied forces were defeating the Axis on all fronts; Field Marshall Montgomery had routed General Rommel in North Africa, General Patton was battling his way through Italy and Germany, and General Eisenhower was trying to beat the Soviets in a race to Berlin. Hitler did not count on a second front in the West. With the German army retreating and defeated in the East, and the Allies bombarding German cities and military installations, Hitler turned to his Luftwaffe for exacting vengeance. Having learned his lesson about sending manned bombers over London, Hitler sent his newly developed unmanned flying bombs, V-1s ("V" for *Vergeltungswaffe,* meaning "weapon of retaliation") across the English Channel. We called them "doodlebugs." The engines of these flying bombs hummed loudly until the engine stopped, sending the bomb into a nosedive. Hearing the hum gave us a chance to take cover and even calculate the arc the doodlebug would take on its way down. Some of these flying bombs were actually shot out of the sky by English Spitfires (fighter planes) because of their slower speed. When this strategy also failed, Hitler launched the V-2s from across the English Channel. These weapons, however, were supersonic rockets which we could not hear coming. We first heard the explosion when they hit the ground, then the whoosh of their dive. No time to run for cover or to calculate where the rocket would hit. England had no air defense against them; the R.A.F. could only try to knock them out at their launching pads across the Channel.

Sam, who had slept through much of the bombing during the London Blitz and had never gone to a shelter, maintained that if a bomb had his name on it, it could hit him in the shelter, too. But he was not really fatalistic; he simply believed he would survive. Indeed he did. During this second bombing blitz, Sam again was as sanguine as before, but this time perhaps he had additional justification: he could predict—from the V-1's sound—when the rocket was not likely to fall near him. With the V-2s, however, all bet were off.

Germany's unconditional surrender was what Churchill, Roosevelt, and Stalin had demanded—a victory that the Allied forces and home fronts had longed for, sacrificed for, and died for. The end (of the war in Europe) came at last on 8 May 1945. I was then still living then with the Crummenerls, and working for the L.M.S. I had finished my matriculation, but could not bring myself to join the raucous, exuberant celebration of the end of the war in Europe—which my parents and Betti had not survived. I also had just learned that my stay in England was "temporary," a status which appeared in my original documents, but I had forgotten. Officially, I had been a stateless refugee and resident, but not an immigrant. I was now 21 years old, the war was over, and I had to move on.

9. From London To America (1946-____)

My traveling papers came in short order. I had the option of going to Palestine or to the U.S., because my Uncle Harry and Simon had provided the necessary affidavit, while my family in Palestine had obtained for me the Certificate. I had struggled earlier making a decision, and had considered the advice I got from Sam and from my sisters in Palestine. I concluded that America was the better option, and my resolution was confirmed. It greatly eased my conscience when the Refugee Children Movement advised me to yield the Certificate for Palestine. This organization that had brought me over on the Kindertransport from Poland told me that if I did not use my Certificate it would be given to another refugee or survivor still in a camp in Europe. After all, I had the opportunity to go to America and join my brother and my relatives. I suspect that the prospect of life in America weighed more heavily in my mind at the time than my imagined future in Israel, notwithstanding my Zionist passion.

Sam was still in the British army, and was stationed somewhere in the Southeast of England, not far from London. Simon, who had finished his U.S. army service by accepting an interpreter's job at the Nuremberg trials, had finished also that assignment and was ready to return to the U.S. by way of London. My itinerary called for going to Glasgow by train, and then by boat to Norfolk, VA. On 26 April 1946, a year after WW II ended in Europe, I was at the Euston railroad station in London, waiting for the train, when Sam and Simon showed up! The most unlikely reunion at the most unlikely place! It was not totally unexpected, however, since we had tried to coordinate our plans. Yet this seemed like another miracle. We three brothers had not been together since 1938. We had only 10 minutes, just enough time to say hello and good-bye. I knew I would see Simon in New York and we would travel together to Chicago. What I didn't know was whether I would see Sam again. (I saw him once more, many years later.)

I noted in my diary that this brief happy moment shared by us, three brothers, was seen by other passengers on the station platform, and it "must have gladdened [their] hearts ... if only they knew ...." I boarded the train, settled in my seat and, having no distractions, reflected on the moves in my young life: Was this trip the end of my life as a refugee or just another phase in my wanderings? The train ride took six to eight long hours, chugging northwest through the night to its destination. Arriving at St. Enoch station in Glasgow, tired and frustrated, I confided in my diary, my "parting wrath at the whole railroad company for which I had once done so much, so long, for so little."

At the Glasgow docks, I boarded the H.M.S. Chaser. It was no passenger liner. It was an American lend-lease aircraft carrier that had seen action during the war under the British flag, and was now being returned to the U.S. But not only was the ship itself being returned, so were the damaged airplanes that were lined up on the flight deck. However, those airplanes never made it back, they were destined for a watery grave. While crossing the Atlantic, which is

H.M.S Chaser

not known for any smooth sailing, the ship bobbed up and down and sideways like a buoy in a rocky bay. As the ship tipped from port to starboard, the sailors removed the chucks from under the airplane wheels to allow the planes to roll off the deck into the sea. What a sorry sight to see these fighter planes disappear among the waves. I clambered onto a bulge of the deck that once housed an anti-aircraft gun and took pictures of one of the planes being dumped. Shooting pictures even from that angle was the easy part. Struggling not to get seasick in this heaving sea was the tough part. (I didn't get sick.

British Warplanes Being Ditched (my photos)
May 1946

My journey to America in some ways recalled my previous sea voyage at age 14 on Kindertransport from Gdynia (Poland) to London. On my earlier voyage, I was with a group of boys—yet I felt alone. Although we had been together in Otwock for four weeks and for another week on board the M/S "Warszawa," it did not lead to any bonding. I could not fathom what lay ahead of me. I was still a kid and knew only that I would be taken care of. The counselors of The Refugee Children's Movement, who were always with us, had virtually assumed parental responsibilities and had looked after us.

And now, seven years after my stay in Great Britain, at age 21, I found myself again on the high seas facing an unknown future. I had become a young adult, more educated by what I had learned from life than from my studies, yet still a naïf on the outside and an orphan on the inside. However, having survived the adversities I encountered in my teenage years, I had developed some confidence in myself. I did not know what awaited me in America, but I felt my trials would be over.

Reflecting on my journey, I was often troubled by a paradoxical thought. Had I not been forcibly expelled from Germany ahead of Kristallnacht, and had I not had the good fortune in Poland to join the Kindertransport, I certainly would not have survived the war. I wondered: did my traumatic deportation and subsequent separation from my parents have a silver lining? Was this turn of events the result of lucky coincidences or predetermined by some higher power? And though I cannot ever know whom to thank for my good fortune, should I not plan my new life to include some restitution?

The accommodations on board the HMS "Chaser" were, of course, for sailors, not for travelers. The ship had only a skeleton crew. I and several other young refugees who came with me slept in the "cabins," which were more like large dorms with 5-tiered bunk beds. There was as much comfort aboard as one would expect to find in a submarine. It didn't really matter; the nine days at sea went by quickly and with great expectations. Because the "HMS Chaser" was still a naval vessel we did not sail into the New York harbor, but we saw the Statue of Liberty at a distance as we passed by. It was an exhilarating moment of welcome without words. This is the *Goldene Medineh*, the country which so many tried to reach, the land that we, refugees, could come to call home. How appropriate the words emblazoned on the statue's pedestal:

> Send these, the homeless, tempest-tossed, to me: I lift my lamp beside the golden door.

We arrived in Norfolk, Virginia, at the American naval base. No crowds awaited us, and there was no reception. Only a Yiddish-language newspaper reported our arrival with a column the next day. We were at last thankfully on our own, and what a relief! And what a joy! We were guided to the railroad station where I took the train to New York to wait for Simon's return to the States. In New York I stayed briefly with the family Gumprecht, friends of Simon. Having been so used to food and clothes rationing, I could only stare in wonder at all that was now available to me.

I had now completed the journey my father undertook back in 1908, but had never finished. Was I destined to complete it? My wandering had ended and a new life had begun.

MAP OF MY JOURNEY

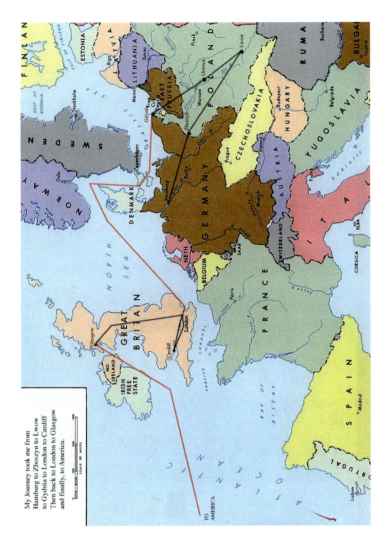

My Journey took me from Hamburg to Zboszyn to Lwow to Gydnia to London to Cardiff Then back to London to Glasgow and finally, to America.

EPILOGUE

After Simon's arrival in New York, we flew to Chicago, where I met Uncle Harry and Aunt Bessie for the first time. Uncle Harry was an easy man to like. With his broad forehead, adorned with receding white hair, and his blue eyes, he had a quiet charisma about him. He was gentle and unassuming. Aunt Bessie made a strong impression. Attractive, tall and slender, she had a central position in her large family circle. She was very caring, and confident of her ability to help others and to solve their problems. I received a very warm welcome and their home became also mine.

A little over three months after I arrived in Chicago, I received a letter with the familiar "Greetings" from the U.S. Department of State. It ordered me to report for induction into the U.S. Army, but with the option to decline because I was not (yet) an American citizen. I was glad to serve, however; I had gained a very positive picture of the American army in London. The war in the Far East as well as in Europe had ended many months earlier and I was in no danger of seeing any fighting. I was inducted at Fort Sheridan, Illinois, and two weeks later went to Fort Belvoir, Virginia, for training as an engineer. There I learned to dig and build field latrines and various other technical "specialties." The incongruity of my reflective nature with the new mindless, rough and tumble army life was challenging. Yet I followed orders and learned to keep up with my buddies when falling out or on forced marches. Songs kept us going. I awakened to the tune of "Oh, how I hate to get up in the morning," and, on the forced marches, I chanted with the rest of the company: "You had a good home and you left, you're right...one, two, one, two...."

My training completed, I was deployed to Korea. I had hoped to be sent to Germany where I could parade in my American army uniform and, perhaps, have an opportunity to find an ex-Nazi I could confront. I tried to convince the deployment officer to send me to Europe, based on my knowledge of German and French—but to no avail. That was not how the army operated. I was bound for what was still in the fall of 1946 the Pacific Theater of Operation. (At the end of WWII in the Pacific, Korea had been liberated from Japanese occupation and the U.S. troops replaced the Japanese.)

In the winter of 1946-47, after a two-week voyage on a troop ship across the Pacific, we landed at Inchon and proceeded to Seoul, the capital of Korea, where I was stationed. Our assignment was to guard the trains carrying supplies to the several American army outposts in South Korea. Riding in those open-door cargo cars in the bitter cold with only a Bunsen burner to keep my hands warm was not my idea of serving my country. So I invented the position of administering the "dayroom" (reading and recreation room) and successfully obtained the company officer's blessing. I then functioned as our unit's Information and Education Specialist until my discharge. I left the army in May 1947 with one stripe on my sleeve and two ribbons on the chest of my Ike jacket. I got my discharge after only 9 months of service, thanks to the Congress's effort to release all draftees at that time. (I was considered a draftee.)

Back in Chicago I made good use of the G. I. Bill. I attended Roosevelt College (now Roosevelt University) and graduated in 1950 with a B. A. in psychology. During my freshman year at Roosevelt I met a fellow student who became my best friend, Lothar Moulton. (Later I rented a room at his parents' apartment near the U of C campus.) He, too, was a German Jewish refugee. His parents had been passengers on the M/S St. Louis. This tragic ship, filled with Jews fleeing the Nazis, was turned away from every port (including the U.S. ports) and was forced to return to Germany, where death awaited them. My friend's parents, however, were an exception; they were lucky enough to have papers that allowed them to get off the ship at Havana, and then travel to the United States. Lothar introduced me to his large circle of friends, including girls whom I dated. When he graduated college, went into business, and married, our paths diverged and, to my everlasting regret, we lost contact.

During those three years in college, I worked part time in the office of a tobacco jobber, where I once broke the bookkeeping machine in my impatience to master it. I enjoyed working there, but wanted to go to graduate school.

I applied for admission to the University of Chicago ("U. of C.") and was accepted into the Ph.D. program in Human Development. One of my professors, who taught several of my classes, was the highly respected and controversial Dr. Bruno Bettelheim. His theory of human development was hotly contested on campus and, more generally, in the field of child psychology. Although he had a reputation for being tough on students, I had a good relationship with him. He supervised me in my work as a counselor at the U. of C.'s residential school for disturbed children where he was the director. "Bruno," as we insiders called him, taught us as much about ourselves as about our little charges. His insights served me well in my growth and in my later work with patients.

My Student ID Card
From The U. of C.

In 1950 I received a stipend from the State of Illinois for two years of study toward the master's degree, which obligated me, following my graduation in 1952, to work in a State Mental Health Center. I remember the day my supervisor encouraged me to continue my studies for the Ph. D. Having fulfilled my obligation at the Center, I returned to the U. of C. for my third year of graduate school, and began working on my dissertation.

In the summer of 1952, I traveled by boat to Israel for my summer vacation to visit my family. Cilli's husband was a steward on the Israeli passenger liner S/S "Jerusalem," and I was only too glad to be on board with him. I was thrilled to see again my two sisters, Cilli and Edith, for the first time in over 14 years. I also was excited to get to know my nephew and two nieces; Edith's little children, Uri, Ilana, and Esti (who now have adult children and grandchildren of their own). I have visited them all many times since then.

In 1985 my brothers, Simon and Julius, and I were reunited for the first time with our sisters, Cilli and Edith, who travelled from Israel to Chicago for my daughter's wedding. In January 2009 my son,

At Betty's Wedding, Chicago, 1985
Standing (from left) Julius, Me, Simon
(Sitting) Edith & Cilli

daughter, and their families joined Edith and her family in Israel for her 90th birthday celebration. Her loving, large and growing family surrounded her, including her 13 great-grandchildren. Of course, my sisters and other members of my Israeli family also came to the States from time to time to visit. Neither the years nor the thousands of miles have diminished our connectedness.

I met my wife, Celia Freemond, in 1955 in Chicago and we raised our family mostly in the suburb of Lincolnwood, Illinois. We first met on a blind date.

As I was preparing for my oral exams that year, a friend called me to say that he knew of a "nice Jewish girl," and asked whether I would be interested to meet her. He suggested that I not take the date too seriously, however, saying "she is not your type." But he was wrong. Celia was a highly intelligent, intuitive, and warm woman, the only child of Romanian Jewish immigrants. Born in Chicago, and raised on Chicago's West Side, she was also educated at the University of Chicago. A licensed clinical social worker with the Jewish Family Service when I met her, she was helping new immigrants get settled and adjusted to their new country. We hit it off on our first date, and by our second date we knew that we would marry.

Simon & Hannah, Me & Celia, Julius & Irma
My Wedding In Chicago, 1956

Our wedding took place on January 29, 1956, in a German Jewish synagogue ("Habonim") on Chicago's south side near the U. of C. campus. After a honeymoon trip to New Orleans, Celia made sure that I would complete my dissertation and start earning enough to support a family.

I obtained my Ph.D. in September 1960, and took a position as clinical psychologist with the Irene Josselyn Clinic (now the Josselyn Health Center), where I worked for the next 20 years as chief psychologist. I also had a private practice, seeing patients in the evenings and on weekends, ultimately at my home office.

Celia and I shared our love for our work and respected each other's expertise. Most gratifying for me were the times when we consulted on cases with each other, or teamed up for the conjoint therapy of a marital couple or for the diagnostic evaluation of a school child.

Back in September 1958 we had a daughter, whom we named Elizabeth, but called Betty (after my sister). In June 1961, we had a son, Edward, whom we called Edo after my older brother who died as a teenager. Ed's middle name is Chaim, after my father. Both kids attended the University of Michigan where they met their spouses before launching their careers. Betty, like her mother and me, became a psychotherapist, and put her career on hold to raise her children. Like her aunt and namesake, Betty is warm, down-to-earth, and strong-minded. Ed, who became a lawyer, honed his ability to argue his case while growing up at home. Celia and I were blessed with four grandchildren;

Me With Celia, Betty And Ed
Lincolnwood, 1970

Aliza and Zoe (Feder), and Ari and Shoshana (Rice). When Aliza was barely a year old, Betty held her as Celia and I walked to our car at the end of a visit. Aliza turned, reached out her arms to me, and to everyone's surprise, said: "Abba." I looked at Betty, smiled, and said: "I've been named." I was only too happy to accept this new name that Aliza had given me. I didn't care for "zeyde" or "grandpa," and "Abba" is Hebrew for "father." That name has stuck to this day; my kids, their spouses, and my grandchildren all call me Abba. And Celia loved nothing better than being "Bubbie" to her grandchildren, who were her heart and soul.

In the summer of 1972, when our kids were young teens, we went on a vacation, which included a trip to Hamburg. I wanted to show my wife and children where I grew up. I also wanted to see if I could recapture some of my repressed feelings about my early life. Our first stop was the Talmud Tora Schule, my alma mater.

The building had survived Kristallnacht and the war intact. No wonder. It had been taken over by the Nazis for the vocational education of the German youth. We came in the late afternoon when the school was already closed and the gate was shut. Not wanting to disappoint my children, I climbed over the gate to find a way in. The caretaker heard me coming, emerged from the building, and asked what I was doing. I explained to him in German that I wanted to show my family where I spent my first 8 years in school. Silently and without hesitation he unhooked a huge ring of keys from his belt, handed them to me, and told me I could open any door I wanted.

As we gingerly made our way down the corridors, I had hoped to recapture some of my childhood feelings. I wanted to experience again what it was like to sit in that class as a boy, loving to learn and—yes—fearing the teacher. A sense of vague familiarity came back to me but, on the whole, I felt disappointed. Of course, much had changed over the nearly 50 years. When I returned the keys to the caretaker, he told me that many other former students had come back to visit the school. And what impact, he wanted to know, had my visit made on me? Not very much, I was sorry to say.

During the 1970s Celia and I worked hard at our practices and raised our kids, in addition to taking care of Celia's aging and ailing parents. In the 1980s, with the kids grown and out of the house, we continued devoting our lives to our work. Then, in

December 1990, most unexpectedly, our lives were shaken: Celia was diagnosed with non-Hodgkin's lymphoma, and was immediately hospitalized with an uncertain prognosis. With months of aggressive chemotherapy, Celia went into remission, but Damocles' sword hung over us. From that time on she struggled with anxiety, and over the years her health began to decline from other chronic conditions. Notwithstanding her increasing physical challenges, Celia maintained her private practice, even to the time when I had to wheel her into our home office, trailing her attached oxygen. None of her clients seemed perturbed by her physical limitations; they wanted to see Celia and would not be distracted by her condition.

In the fall of 2003 I received an invitation from Hamburg's city administration to revisit the town of my birth. It was part of a statewide project to make amends with former Jewish citizens of German towns, who presumably still had bitter memories of the life they had led there. My son, Ed, was able to join me, while my daughter, Betty, cared for Celia, easing my conscience about

My Return Visit To Hamburg 2003 In Front Of The Talmud Tora

having to leave her for a week. In Hamburg, along with other Jewish refugees and their guests, we were shown great hospitality and treated royally with sight-seeing tours, banquets, and performances with the best seats in the house. In addition to providing our flights, hotel, and meals, our hosts even supplied us with German marks for spending money. Ed and I enjoyed our own private explorations more than the programmed agenda. We went to the Grindel and checked out the apartment house at Grindelhof 8 where our family had lived. It looked unchanged, except that it had been repainted and, of course, our name, Zloczower, was no longer listed at the entrance. I was half-inclined to ring the bell for the second floor, wondering if the old apartment, too, had remained the same. But I thought the better of it.

We took time out of our busy agenda to visit the graves of my brothers, Moritz and Edo, in Ohlsdorf, outside of Hamburg. We found the old Jewish cemetery, overgrown with weeds and with crumbling headstones, untouched by war or vandalism. When Ed stood at Edo's grave, he seemed to be virtually in a trance, as if trying to imagine his uncle's life. He almost missed the bus that would take us back to the hotel. After I returned home, I arranged to have the old headstones replaced by new ones.

In our group each participant briefly told his story. I discovered that I was the only one who had been forcibly deported to Poland. Others had left Germany for England on the Kindertransport, or with their parents, or somehow on their own. One woman, who heard my story, asked me after my short talk, "How did you maintain your identity when you left Germany, came to Poland, went to England, and ended up in America?" I told her I had no problem with my identity: I was a Jew wherever I went; always a Jew, first and foremost.

I found myself wondering about the Jewish identity of the other members in our group. We all had felt the Nazis' boot for one reason only: we were Jewish or were considered Jewish. For Yom Kippur, which fell in the middle of our visit, the organizers had thoughtfully arranged for a cab to take anybody so inclined, to the local synagogue for services. Yet only one couple out of our group of 30 (besides Ed and me) accepted that offer. Reflecting on this "no show," I was troubled by the thought that on that holiest of our Holy Days, my fellow ex-patriots had other plans. In America even non-observant Jews attend Yom Kippur services out of a sense of their Jewish identity.

The service was conducted by the *chazzan*, a Russian immigrant, who read all prayers in Hebrew at a rate so rapid that I could not follow him. Another Russian, sitting across the aisle from me, saw my dilemma and came over, showing me where we were on the page. For a moment I felt as if I were back in our own little shul with my Papa helping me navigate the Hebrew prayer book.

Over the next several years, Celia became increasingly incapacitated. Our family rallied to keep her at home between her stays at the hospital and rehabilitation centers. Though homebound, she followed everything that was happening in the family and elsewhere. She remained alert and kept her own unique and perverse sense of humor to everyone's delight, while we continued to hope that she would be with us longer. I devoted myself to caring for Celia. I closed my private practice in her last year, and had no further need to function, or be identified, as a clinical psychologist. I resigned from the professional organizations, donated my journals, shredded my records, and would not use my title again. In February 2007 Celia died peacefully in her sleep. She was the flame that lit up our lives, but also on occasion burned us a little. I then devoted myself to another, different life of retirement, and began writing my story.

APPENDIX A: More Family Reminiscences

I have still many more memories of my brothers and sisters from my early childhood, as well as from my adult and later life. Although I have finished recording my journey, I do not want these additional thoughts and vignettes to be lost. Hopefully they will illuminate what I already have written. However, I need to limit my recollections to my immediate family, past and present. I will leave a narrative of my life with my grandchildren, nephews and nieces to a biographer of another generation.

Eighteen years older than I, Sam was my "big brother." During my growing up at home, he was the disciplinarian who believed in the German precept that children should be seen but not heard. There was one world for adults, and another for children. He was guided by what he knew about German pedagogy, prevalent at the time. Looking back years later, I have come to understand that my mother, who was disillusioned early in her marriage, had elevated Sam to the position of paterfamilias, a role that my

Sam In Hamburg, 1938

father had failed to assume. I imagined my mother must have turned to Sam for advice on financial matters and for any dealings with authorities. Although my mother did not hold him up as a role model for me to follow, he was considered the most important member of our family.

I saw Sam in my childhood as a disciplinarian, strict but never punitive. I remember that he would not allow Betti and me to play cards lest we turn into card sharks. Betti and I had miniature playing cards that came in small packages of candy, which we could easily hide whenever we were in danger of being caught playing with them. When Sam did catch us, he would simply take the cards away.

I don't recall Sam or my parents ever scolding me, let alone slapping me, which was common back then. By contrast, the withholding of privileges or being sent to one's room was not part of our culture. But then, I never caused any trouble at home other than frustrating my mother with my finicky eating. Moreover, I sensed the unspoken family dictum: Don't rock the boat.

However, I must confess I was a little sneaky at times, probably like many other boys my age. Sam had things at home that I coveted, like the halvah that he had in a tin can on a shelf in his room. When he was out of the house, I stole in his room, carefully helped myself to a few spoonful, and made sure to smoothen the surface of the halvah. He never detected my little thievery, and I never felt guilty about it. After all, I figured he could have offered me some. He never noticed it.

Except for such incidents at home, Sam and I lived separate lives. My mother's constant concern for my health led her to persuade Sam on one occasion to take me along on an outing for some fresh air and fun. I went with him and his group of friends to a beach in Blankenese, a vacation spot on the river Elbe near Hamburg. I enjoyed myself being the center of attention and in Sam's care ... an experience I had again only several years later.

Sam (with the cigarette)
And I On The Beach At Blankenese, ca. 1937

When I came to live in London (1941-1946), I got to know another side of Sam. He became more of a big brother to me. Though I did not live with him, we spent some time together. He was divorced and had enlisted in the British army. (As a Polish national, Sam was required to report to the Free Polish Army in England, but had the option to enlist in the British forces instead.) Sam officially changed his name, as many other Jewish soldiers did, in order to conceal their religious identity should they be captured by the Germans. Sam adopted the name "Eden", after Anthony Eden, the British foreign minister whom he admired. Sam served in Britain and did not see any action. However, he wrote he was lonely and longed to be with me, his one brother in our dispersed family. My image of Sam changed. I felt he had become a friend to me.

Many years after the war, I visited Sam with my family on a nostalgic trip to London. By that time he was in a late stage of Parkinson's disease. Fortunately he had earlier remarried a physician who took good care of him. With his death a year or two after my visit, our family lost its anchor in England, and I lost the man who was once my remote idol, my guardian, my companion, and ultimately the big brother I came to love.

Like Sam, my oldest sister, Cilli, was already out of the house when I was born. Thankfully for her, I was the last baby she had to help out with at home. Only years later she told me she was not too thrilled to be mother's little helper as baby after baby came along. All my brothers and sisters who came before me had benefitted from her being a little mother to them.

Cilli worked for a well-to-do Jewish attorney in Hamburg as his secretary. Her boss was quite a philanthropist who took on our family as his personal charity case. My mother spoke of him with great respect and gratitude. From our benefactor I got a pair of ice skates, but I never learned to skate and I never used them. One day I got a used bicycle, which also may have been a gift from our donor. It was a little too big for me, so I learned to ride it standing up, and I happily rode it up and down the bicycle path on the Grindelallee. I have always thought of that bicycling experience as emblematic of much that I have had to learn in my life: the hard way.

I remember also the time a Jewish seaman, by the name of Sally Schieber, came to see us and to call on Cilli in 1931. He had sailed from Buenos Aires and brought greetings from our family in Argentina. In retrospect, I imagine my aunt Fanny had told him of Cilli's beauty and availability. Not known for any shy-ness, Sally took no time to woo and marry Cilli. He had a lively personality and loved to joke and clown. He and my Uncle Munio would have made quite a comedy duo. When he told me he had played soccer on a Buenos Aires team, we instantly became pals.

I was 8 years old when Cilli and Sally married in 1932. The first of her two girls, Inge, was born a year later and I was proud to be already an uncle. When Inge (she changed her name later in Israel to Yehudit) was 2 years old and I not quite 11, I was charged one afternoon with being her babysitter. I took that opportunity to see what that grown-up stuff about smoking cigarettes was all about. I filched a cigarette from

Cilli And Her Daughter, Inge
Haifa, 1936

Sam's room, lit it, and took a puff. I nearly choked. That was no fun. With the second puff I resolved never to smoke again.

I got to feel much closer to Cilli in my adult years when I came to visit her. It was a trip back in time for me when I sat at her kitchen table and enjoyed the *heymishe* (homey) dishes she prepared for me (like "lungen," beef lung, which my mom used to make back in Hamburg). Cilli was known in our family as very competent and efficient. She seemed to have clearly taken after our mother. And like our mother, Cilli always maintained a positive outlook in spite of adverse experiences.

Cilli lived a full life in Israel long after Sally had passed away. Even as an octogenarian Cilli worked in a tourist gift shop after she had moved to Eilat. Her selling and social skills amazed both her coworkers and her customers. She even made the news in a local newspaper that applauded her work and her undaunted longevity. She had eased well into her nineties when I visited her in the hospital for the last time. She had made her peace with her life. When she passed away at age 99, a giant in our family had fallen.

Just like my relationship with Sam, Simon and I lived separate lives in Hamburg. Eleven years older than I, Simon was never in my world when I was a kid. By the time I was in second grade he, like Sam, was out of the house and working. When he was home, I loved to watch him play chess with Sam or with our family friends, the Schainowsky brothers. He was devoted to chess all his life; he enjoyed analyzing masters' games and doing chess puzzles. I shared his love of chess. When the time came for Simon to leave Hamburg in 1938, he gave me his stamp collection, which I didn't even know he had. His gift was a great addition to my own collection, but I had only a month to enjoy it before I, too, had to leave it behind.

In the eight years after he left Hamburg (and before he and I were reunited in America), Simon and I corresponded. His letters already showed the interest he would take in my new life with him. He worked for a family-owned coffee company as a branch manager, and was well-liked. He trained others to move up the executive ladder and never expressed any regrets over not having moved up himself. Nor was he competitive with his trainees who did. His gentle nature accepted what fate dealt him. When I came to see him in his office shortly after my arrival in Chicago, he introduced me to the owner of the firm who asked me how I had found my way to the coffee plant. "No problem," I told him, "I simply followed the smell of the coffee." The owner was greatly amused and was ready to offer me a job in his advertising department.

Simon At
Continental Coffee
Chicago, 1938

Simon developed a close and caring relationship with me. He was engaged in my life. We shared an apartment before he got married. He took pride in my academic progress. In fact, he underwrote my living expenses with monthly deposits when I was in college and could work only part time. He called those deposits to me "loans," but when the time came that I could repay him, he tore up all my checks.

Julius, Simon And Me At Simon's wedding
New York, 1949

Simon married a young, beautiful woman of Jewish Hungarian background. She was a teenager when the Nazis seized her. She was imprisoned in a concentration camp where she suffered bitterly. Fortunately she was rescued at the end of the war and sent to neutral Sweden to recuperate from all she had to endure. Simon's and Hana's traumatic past stayed in the background and rarely came to the fore. Hana was a true survivor, but could not talk about the past in Simon's presence. He could not bear to hear of it; it was too painful for him, too. I sensed that, without realizing it, Simon still was suffering from what the Nazis had done to our parents.

After they had married, Simon and Hana adopted a pretty, blonde baby girl whom they named Regina, or "Reggie," and raising their daughter became a new focus for their life. Reggie was a happy, strong-minded little girl who did not always take her dad's disciplinary measures seriously. One day I took Reggie on a ride in my car. I don't recall much about the outing. However, I remember her sitting in the backseat behind me, as I was driving, and repeatedly kicking the back of my seat. Since my asking her to stop it had no effect, I stopped the car and removed her shoes. The ride proceeded without any further trouble. I know Reggie has remembered that incident to this day.

When he was old enough to retire, Simon moved to San Diego with Hana and Reggie, where he spent the rest of his years. I kept in close contact with him and visited him from time to time. I remember how in one of my trips Simon took me through his newly purchased house (he moved several times, much to the dismay of Hana) and proudly showed me his collection of classical CDs and his many books. It seemed as if he took greater pleasure in his well—indexed music than in listening to it. And I could relate to his delight in organization. I came to realize that Simon was identified with me and I with him. We shared many interests and most importantly, we were involved in each other's lives. When Simon died on Christmas 2008 at the age of 95 I felt his loss deeply. His brotherly love and his generosity will always stay with me.

Next in line was Julius, just a year younger than Simon. Julius told me that he remembered the time I was born, and how thrilled he was to have a baby brother. Whereas I was a very conforming child, Julius was a bit of a maverick. No doubt, Julius took after our father in looks and temperament. He was handsome, outgoing, and not as conforming or compliant as the rest of us.

When he was five or six years old he took a 20-mark bill from our mother's hiding place and tried to buy candy with it. The candy store owner was suspicious, seeing a little kid with so much money. He wheedled from little Julius his address and told his parents what happened. The jig was up. I don't know whether Julius got any candy, but he got a rare whipping.

On occasion Julius devised another way to get some money. He importuned people on the street with a sob story about having lost his money to buy a cigar for his dad, and said that he was terrified of receiving a beating if he went home without it. People would then take pity on him and give him a few pfennige. Or he would slip into the local movie theater through the backdoor when others came out. He was clearly the least docile of all of us. I loved and admired him for it, but I also envied him for his undaunted spirit.

After leaving school, Julius had been apprenticed to a furrier. He set up a workshop, a small triangular room at the back of our apartment in Hamburg. I loved to hang around and watch him work with his pelts. He would first nail the wet fur skins to a board, let them dry out, and then cut them to a pattern. He would sew the skins together with what looked like a funny sewing machine—not like the one my mother used to mend our clothes. Learning the fur trade was of little use to him when he immigrated to Palestine, but it was the foundation of his career when he came to America.

Julius
About 1936

Julius got out of Germany in 1935 or 1936, at age 21, by signing on with a Jewish Palestinian shipping company. His ship plied between Haifa and Constanta, a Romanian Black Sea port. As I learned later, the separation from our parents and home was very difficult and painful for him. When he changed his seagoing life for one on land in Palestine, he lived in a kibbutz with other Jewish "pioneers" from Germany. Julius had several different jobs there. For a time, he was a policeman who patrolled on horseback. At other times, he worked in the community kitchen, or played accordion in the bars. He caught the eye of a petite, vivacious, dark-haired and dark-eyed immigrant girl from Germany,

Tamara Stern (who later changed her first name back to Irma). She fell in love with Julius and married him before any other girl could get to him. Julius adored her and loved her all his life.

Julius and Irma left Israel with their two young boys, Ronnie and Gary (originally Roni and Gadi) around 1948, after a part of Palestine was declared a Jewish state. Irma had difficulty adjusting to the difficult living conditions in Israel at that time, so the family set out for America. Once again, Aunt Bessie came through for the Zloczowers, and prepared a rental apartment for the new arrivals, fully furnished, complete with all necessary household equipment and foodstuffs in the kitchen cabinets. All Julius and his young family had to do was to move in.

When the family arrived in Chicago, I quickly got to know my young nephews. On my second date with Celia I had asked her to come and babysit Julius's boys with me. Little Gary had the TV on and was watching Deanna Durbin, a pretty, popular female singer. On being introduced to my new date, our pipsqueak, Gary, pointed to the lovely lady on the screen and announced to Celia that *she* (the woman on TV) was my girlfriend. (I had to be careful around him.) I also have a fun memory of Ronnie as a young boy. When he was in second or third grade, he gave me as a gift a pair of leather cuff links, which he had made in school. I made sure to wear them on my next visit. Ronnie noticed and said, with what I considered a precocious understanding, "Uncle Gunther, you don't need to wear the cuff links to show me that you like them."

Soon after his arrival in the States, Julius was able to take up again his trade for which he had been trained. He opened a successful fur shop in Evanston, a Chicago suburb, and worked hard as the owner, salesman, and shopkeeper. He made a luxurious black, soft and shiny fur coat for me with red silk lining and my name sewn in. I still have it, but it doesn't fit me anymore. It is one of my precious possessions. I must admit, however, I could neither bring myself to wear it nor to part with it.

When Julius decided to retire, he sold his store and moved with his wife to San Diego, joining Simon and his family. He had a comfortable, modest ranch home with a garden he tended with pride. (I was amazed to see an orange tree onto which a lemon branch had been grafted, and both bearing fruit.) He also had a backyard patio where I played table tennis with him when I visited. California was his paradise. He so wanted me to move to San Diego, and he was rather insistent. I toyed with the idea for a time, but one look at the numerous psychologists listed in the local phone book convinced me that my resettling there was not a good idea professionally. Eventually Julius accepted my remaining in Chicago and my visiting him as often as I could. As he grew older, Julius suffered from Parkinson's disease, like our older brother, Sam. He then moved to a retirement home where he died in 1996 at the age of 82. That was a painful loss. It left my sister, Edith, and me as the last of the original Zloczower clan.

Edith was, and is, my favorite sister. Only five years older than I, she spent time with me when I was a kid, and those times were for me unmitigated joy. No quarreling, no fighting. Quarreling was more typical of my relationship with Betti. I was always, even today in my senior years, Edith's little brother. I felt her love, and my love for her was totally unreserved.

I remember one particular day when Edith and I went out on the town in Hamburg. I rarely ventured out of our neighborhood, so this outing promised to be quite an adventure. We didn't have far to go to get into the city center where all kinds of travelers and foreigners mixed with the locals. We pretended to be tourists, and recited in Hebrew whatever phrases or songs we could think of, as if we were conversing in some strange tongue. Edith might say *"adon olam ..."* and I would answer *"asher malakh ...."* This lasted until we reached the periphery of our own neighborhood. What great fun that was for a homebound, provincial boy!

If teasing is a sign of love, Edith was an expert: she showed it in many ways. She would gently kid me in order to make her surprises more exciting. I'll never forget the day she brought home some postage stamps and asked me whether they had any value. I was an avid stamp collector by then and was ready to give her my opinion. She laid the stamps out in a row on my bed and said she wanted to give them to her boyfriend, Milo, the Talmud Tora student who boarded with us. My eyes popped out with excitement and envy. When I assured her that they were wonderful and valuable stamps, she broke her pretense and said there were really for me.

Edith had managed to get out of Germany in time, thanks to the Women's International Zionist Organization (WIZO), which provided certificates for Jewish girls to make aliyah (immigrate to Palestine). When she got her traveling papers she couldn't wait to show them to Milo on their next date. She took them with her on their long walk in the evening and lost them. Edith and Milo, trying to contain their panic, went out again and retraced their steps, accompanied by a third pair of eyes from someone in our family. It may have been an older brother who went with them and, to everyone's relief, they found the papers. We didn't dare think what might have happened to her had she not recovered the travel documents. When she left home for Palestine I missed her terribly.

Edith, Age 19
Tel-Aviv Beach 1938

I remember a letter Edith wrote from Tel Aviv to my mother in 1939 when I was still in Poland with my

Edith And Her Husband, Shmuel Galili

parents and Betti. In it she described a suitor she had met who was so in love with her and insistent in his courtship. She loved him, too, but as a naive 20-year old girl, she still sought her mother's opinion. She got mother's blessing and married Shmuel Galili, a very paternal businessman. In due course they started a family with a girl, Ilana, a boy, Uri, and another girl, Esti. This three-branched Israeli sapling grew into a large and leafy tree, providing Edith with eight grandchildren, thirteen great-grand-children, and still counting.

Shmuel, an immigrant from Romania, was an unusual man whom I admired and loved. He had an import business for wood-working machines and was a very successful entrepreneur. Knowledgeable and empathic, and with a secure sense of unchanging values, he was the "head" of our Israeli family, and the model of an authoritarian but loving father. And all of his progeny rightfully became the source of his and Edith's pride.

Shmuel was a most generous man, a trait he passed on to his children, from which I benefitted in all my visits to Israel. I have also seen that his generosity was not limited to his family. One day in Israel he took me on a round to his customers, chatting with them and collecting anything due him. One customer, who was unable to pay, did not get any reproach or pressure from Shmuel. He sympathized with the man, encouraged him, and expressed his trust in the man's eventual ability to settle his account. All too aware of American business practices, I was so impressed with my brother-in-law, that I could not forget this ordinary, mundane incident. Shmuel had a hobby of collecting elephants of different materials, designs, and sizes. Like the attributes of these giant creatures, he too was gentle and had great strength.

Edith was a natural with children of all kinds and ages, and loved her work as a kindergarten teacher. As the years passed, she turned her talent and devotion to her own children and to each succeeding generation in her family. In my visits to her, she would overwhelm me with all her loving attention and care. I felt like the prodigal son who had returned home. I was still the "little brother" in her eyes, and the years and the miles that separated us, vanished. And it has remained so to this day. On many of my visits, I noticed that Edith would inadvertently refer to Uri by my name, and also would call me by his name. Uri and Gunther seemed to have come together in her mind. She bestowed her maternal love on both of us. I often wondered what my future would have been like had I elected to go to Palestine in 1946 when I had the choice to do so.

Since Edith started her family at a relatively young age, and since I am five years younger than she, I have always felt as if I belonged to the same generation as her children, my Israeli nieces and nephews. More like a sister than my niece, Ilana shares my thoughts and, I feel, reciprocates my affection for her. At times, she reminds me still of my mother in many ways. She takes on taxing responsibilities for her family, and worries about everyone, particularly her mother. Now a grandmother herself, Ilana gives her full time and energy to tending her grandchildren. Just like my mother, she occasionally lets out a sign of resignation, which endears her to me.

Ilana's husband, Yossi Steinman, is another member of my family's pantheon. I admire his intense intellectuality and his modesty and his passion for collecting cultural artifacts. I look proudly at the calling card he once gave me—years ago, when he was the treasurer of the municipality of Tel Aviv—and think of it as emblematic of the esteem in which I hold him. I remember the time Yossi and Ilana came to the United States with their two little boys and stayed briefly with my family in Lincolnwood, another suburb of Chicago. I was amazed when Yossi took off with his young family on a road trip across the country in their rented car; his adventurous spirit was in such contrast to my overly-cautious attitude.

My nephew, Uri, so resembles his father in both his looks and his protective passion for the family, that I feel as close to him as to his dad.. On my several trips to Israel, Uri, like his father before him, would take me on tours of the country. I cannot forget my visit to Belt Hatfutzot, the Diaspora Museum, where I saw models of destroyed synagogues that once graced the Jewish communities in Europe. As I gazed with amazement at these simulated reconstructions, I became aware of the soft music that was playing in the background: it was a liturgical song I had not heard since I left my home in Germany.

Uri married a beautiful, bright woman also named llana, who is descended from Spanish Jews that were exiled during the Inquisition. I delight in sharing with her my thoughts and feelings about virtually any subject. She is so simpatico. Edith, who is very fond of her daughter-in-law, Ilana, still tells me how well the plant I had once given llana has thrived. More than a compliment to Ilana's green thumb, it somehow feels as if Edith means to say that Ilana's care of the plant symbolically extends to me.

Edith's youngest daughter, Esti, was almost 11 years old when she first came to live with my family in Chicago in the summer of 1967. Like her brother, Uri, who as a teen stayed for a time with Julius and his sons, Esti was expected to perfect her English and to soak up the "American experience." One day we took her to the famed Chicago lakefront with its public and private beaches. She admired the view, but was totally indignant that many stretches of the lakefront were reserved for the homeowners and not open to the public. Her community mindedness collided with our American view of individualism, and young as she was, Esti gave us a good argument. I admired how she never backed away from a challenge, no matter how small. I once bet her when we were on an hours-long sightseeing trip, tired and hungry, that she would be unable to finish a huge dinner that she had ordered at our favorite deli. I lost that bet.

That June Israel went to war with Egypt for six decisive days. We worried terribly about our Israeli family, but Esti remained unperturbed; she was convinced that Israel would win and that her parents and siblings would be safe. I was proud of her utter confidence in Israel's victory. Esti grew up to reach the height of her profession, as the director of Child Psychiatry at Hadassah Hospital. I was particularly proud of her when she went to Sri Lanka after the tsunami to train health workers help the storm-tossed children recover from their trauma. She married a Jungian psychiatrist, Eli Weistub, who had emigrated from Canada, and raised three children; two daughters and a son. Their home in the old section of Jerusalem was for me always a joy to see. And so were the conversations we had about our profession and about politics.

Betti was the sibling I was closest to in age and the one with whom I spent the most time. Barely three years older than I, she was my constant playmate and confidante. I loved her very much, but with just a tinge of resentment for the demands she made which my mother could not or would not meet. She

Betti, Age 16

was a little persistent in wanting this or that, seemingly not concerned about or perhaps unaware of, our indigence. My mother considered her behavior selfish and stubborn, but Betti only asked for things that were perfectly appropriate for her age. She certainly knew how to assert herself, but never caused any real trouble. While I sought to spare my parents, Betti was more insistent on getting her way. She was lively, whereas I was quiet. I confided in her my suppressed feelings, and she kept my secrets. She tried to allay my fear of girls, and clued me in on what girls expect from boys.

Betti blossomed in her teenage years and matured quickly when her life—together with my parents' and mine—was compressed by the ensuing trauma. Reading between the last lines my mother wrote, Betti must have been a great source of comfort and strength to our parents. In Lwow, she contributed to our parents' meager and waning resources, working in a beauty salon, learning the trade and struggling to master some basic phrases in Polish, Ukrainian, and Russian. Yet she was neither discouraged nor deterred by that task. She never failed to add some lines to my mother's letters, and they were always upbeat even when she described the miseries of their everyday life. The last time I saw her I cannot recall. It is irretrievably lost in my mind. Nor can I imagine how she might have looked had she lived beyond her young years. She has always remained my 18-year old sister. I honored my memory of Betti years later by naming my daughter, Betty (Elizabeth), after her.

Betti and me
Hamburg, 1938

APPENDIX B: Translated Correspondence

1. 9 March 1913, Hamburg,
   Fanny to Uncle Harry 168
2. 6 February 1914 Hamburg,
   Nathan to Uncle Harry 171
3. 10 May 1914 Buenos-Aires,
   Nathan to Uncle Harry 172
4. 30 June 1914 Hamburg,
   Fanny to Uncle Harry 173
5. 1 December 1914 Hamburg,
   Mother to Uncle Harry 174
6. 23 January 1915 Hamburg,
   Fanny to Uncle Harry 175
7. 12 March 1915 Hamburg,
   Fanny to Uncle Harry 176
8. 24 November 1915
   Hamburg, Fanny to Uncle Harry 178
9. 25 January 1916 Hamburg,
   Mother to Uncle Harry 180
10. 26 February 1916 Hamburg,
    Fanny to Uncle Harry 182
11. 17 August 1919 Hamburg,
    Fanny to Uncle Harry 183
12. 28 October 1919 Hamburg,
    Fanny to Uncle Harry 185
13. 22 August 1922 Buenos-Aires,
    Nathan to Uncle Harry 187
14. 25 September 1922 Amsterdam,
    Fanny to Uncle Harry 188
15. 26 July 1932 Buenos-Aires,
    Fanny to Uncle Harry 190
16. 24 April 1933 Hamburg,
    Mother to Uncle Harry 192

17.	3 November 1937 Hamburg, Mother to Uncle Harry	195
18.	10 January 1938 Hamburg, Mother to Uncle Harry	199
19.	9 March 1938 Hamburg, Mother to Uncle Harry	200
20.	1 September 1938 Hamburg, Mother to Uncle Harry	204
21.	15 September 1938 Hamburg, Mother to Uncle Harry	206
22.	12 February 1939 Zbaszyn, Mother to Uncle Harry	208
23.	26 July 1939 Lwow, Mother and Others to me	211
24.	2 August 1939 Lwow Mother & Betti to me	213
25.	4 August 1939 Lwow, Mother & Others to me	217
26.	6 August 1939 Lwow, Mother to me	218
27.	8 August 1939 Lwow, Betti to me	220
28.	8 August 1939 London, Sam to the family	223
29.	21 August 1939 Lwow, Mother & Betti to me	235
30.	28 January 1940 Lwow, Mother to me	240
31.	18 October 1940 Lwow, Mother to me	241
32.	18 February 1941 Lwow, Mother to me	242
33.	14 March 1941 Lwow, Mother to me	244

34. 26 August 1942 London,
    Sam to me 245

Letter from Fanny Fruchter to Uncle Harry (in German)
Hamburg, 9 March 1913

My dear Brother Hermann,

Although I have not heard anything from you for such a long time, I will write to you this time. I want to let you know that the letter you had sent to Laura arrived here already long ago. We were all happy that you let us hear something from you. We also got quite concerned that you had to torment yourself. So, how are you doing now? For the bad times you have had, hopefully things will go all the better for you now.

Dear Brother Hersch, what do you say to H... [?] who sailed to Argentina on March 3 from Hamburg. May dear God stand by his side in all his undertakings. He too has not yet had anything good happen to him. God willing he will arrive in Buenos-Aires on March 30. He has written to us everything possible about the ship, but he is getting good food. He also had some violent headaches.

Now, my dear brother, I will let you know the sad news, which you have perhaps already heard. Uncle Abraham Jacob Hausman died in his sleep last month. His wife received 30 Gulden, and Chaye Hausman, Leiser's wife, moved in that house. Her own house, next to Schwitzer [sp?] she rented out. At the same time I can tell you that Aron Waldman had served in the military at Striy and, I believe, has now already been discharged and is free. He still thinks about going to Hamburg. I am still not doing so well. No one advises me to go to America. It could be that one day I might find myself in Argentina.

One thing makes me happy here: I have a great girl friend, namely Cilli, your little sweetheart, am I right? How is your brother Max? Does he also have a sweetheart already? Does he go to the dance of [Yiddish word].... Why don't we hear anything from him? When you see him ask him all those questions. And I wonder also why Morris hasn't answered me, but that you should not ask him that.

Dear brother, I will also ask you whether you know that your dear father has been quite ill for the past 4 weeks. Yossele wrote that a doctor had to come from Striy, and the Chevra Kadishe [?] paid for it. You won't believe how that affected me. We all pray to God he should make a good recovery. He is after all the father of so many children. We hope that dear God in his mercy will soon have him get well.

Dear brother, when you send me your answer don't forget to tell me whether you have received the postcard ... [?] where he has enclosed his letter for you. Since I am tired and it is already late, I will close this letter in the hope that you will soon answer it. You should excuse my poor writing, and I cannot write *faster than I have been doing. So, with warm regards from your sister, Family Fruchter.*

Letter from Nathan Fruchter to Uncle Harry (in Yiddish)
Hamburg, 6 February 1914

Dear Hersh,

How is it that we don't hear anything from you? You have been in Hamburg for a long time and have promised even a ship's passage, and now you don't even say how you are doing. How much are you making a week? What kind of work are you doing? Don't be so lazy, and write clearly. On our part, I have nothing important to report, other than that we are well. Hope to God to hear the same from you. How is Mottele, and the [?] sister. Warm regards to you, Mottele, Sarah, Leah Brayne [sp?] her husband and children, from me. Nathan.

(In German)

Dear Brother Hermann,

I received your card on Rosh Hashana [sic] and lost your address immediately. I also wrote home asking for your address, but have not had any reply while hoping that you are doing pretty well. I can tell you that I was for 13 weeks in Antwerp, Belgium. It was lovely. So, warmest regards from your sister, Fanny.

Note: This postcard does not have a complete address nor a postage stamp. It is most likely that it was enclosed in an envelope.

Postcard from Nathan Fruchter to Uncle Harry (in Yiddish) Buenos-Aires, 10 May 1914

Dear Brother,

I thank you warmly for your postcard. I also was glad to read that you find yourself, thank God, in a good situation. May God grant that we will always hear good news from each other. I am, thank God, well, and am earning as much as I need, but by trading and not by working. I am very glad that your dear father finds himself now, thank God, in good health. I felt hurt when Leah Esther wrote me that he was ill. If it is agreeable to God, we may yet meet happily in Hamburg. I am now writing also a card to your father. So, with warm regards to you, and regards to Moyshe and Sarah and Leah Brayne [sp?] and all relatives and acquaintances, from me, your brother, Nathan.

Please write often, I will always answer you.

Postcard from Fanny to Uncle Harry (in German)
Hamburg, 30 June 1914

Dear Herrman!

After having waited a long time for your letter, I finally received it. Unfortunately, it contained such sad news. I don't believe that you can imagine how this affects me. Only God alone in heaven knows. I wrote immediately to Jakob that he should inquire about father and immediately report to us everything. It is sad enough that we first hear about father's illness from Chicago. We have not heard from Yossele for at least 6 months. Right after I received your postcard I wrote him that he should answer me at once. I want to tell you that Israel Leib Muhlrad went home a week ago. [This is followed by indecipherable words, among which are an address: Zloczower, Lemberg, Zamarstynow ... presumably I.L.Muhlrad went back to Poland]. *Also, Jakob Maas* [?] *is seeing Nathan's sister and insists on getting engaged to her, but Nathan is opposed to it. I'm getting off the month of July and can now get some rest. More next time.*

Heartfelt regards from your sister, Fanny.

Please answer soon. Regards from Cilli.

Postcard from Laura Zloczower to Uncle Harry (in German) Hamburg, 1 December 1914

Dear Brother,

We received your letter yesterday, but it was the first one, not the third one as you said. Perhaps you still have some letters lying about. Now you can no longer get it out. You asked how we are. Thank God, we are quite well. We don't know anything here, in Hamburg, from need. Chaim is so far still working. Of [?] there isn't much either, and many items are a little more expensive. So you have to make do. We have no news from Lemberg, nor from jackets [sp?] or from Jacob; there is simply no mail. Regarding the war, you can read everything in the papers. How are your brothers and sisters? What's new with you? I cannot get out of my mind how your father, sad to say, is doing. It is terrible that no exchange of letters is possible [with Bolechow]. May God protect and help everyone and lead Austria and Germany to victory. Fanny is staying with me, and Cirale is working. When you'll write to us again, I'll send you a letter with more news from us. For now, heartfelt greetings from all of us. Also heartfelt regards for your brothers and sisters from your well-doing Laura Chaim Zloczower, who loves all the little ones.
Special regards from Fanny who waits for an answer [from you]. Regards from Cirale.

Postcard from Fanny Fruchter to Uncle Harry (in German) Hamburg 23 January 1915

Dear Brother Hermann,

I have received your letter already some time ago, for which I am very thankful to you. I am also glad that you had sent me a picture. You look rather bad. Dear Brother, Laura got your letter yesterday, which she will answer shortly. What you had told her about the war, we know here, too. Germany already publishes the whole truth in all newspapers. We often also get newspapers from Buenos-Aires, in fact, Yiddish papers. Here too, groceries are significantly more expensive. The weather isn't pleasant, either. One time it rains, another time it snows. I want to tell you still a minor matter. Laura gave birth to a boy on January 2, with the name Julius. He is the fifth boy. What do you say to that? Also, Chaim was drafted on January 15 [his age, 37] *but was rejected* [no reason stated] *and can no longer be drafted in this war. Otherwise there is nothing more I can write about. If it's no trouble to you and you could send us newspapers, we would be very grateful.*

With best regards and …[?]*, your sister Fanny.*

Letter from Fanny Kauf with Note from Cilli
(in German)
Hamburg, 12 March 1915

Dear Brother Hermann,

I have received your letter as well as the newspaper for which I thank you very much. Again I want to give you some cheerful news, namely, Aron Waldmann has been in Russian captivity since 9 September. We got the news from there on 4 February, we would like to pass this on to his parents! Your son is alive! He is in Siberia. He have sent him 10 M [Marks] *so that he has something for himself. I Unfortunately, the times are very bad, the exchange rate* [sp?] *rises from day to day. I celebrated my 20ʷ birthday on 1 March.* [10 yrs younger than Laura] *We have two Russian Jews where I'm staying and they made me a present of a very big album of picture postcards. If it is not too much trouble for you, send me some time a beautiful card. Am I perhaps too impudent? Well? After all, I have no prospect* [to come to] *Chicago. I have been at Laura's since the 15 November and will stay with her, since I have lost my interest in getting a job. If you want still to send newspapers, you don't need to send them every two days, you can send them once a week with Yiddish additions* [?]. *You have my best thanks in advance. Last week we received a letter from Nathan. Things are going very badly for him. He incurred a lot of debts, and he doesn't even have a small income. He doesn't know what to do, and so he is in ....* [?] *And I cannot now help him. I would like to ask you why your brother Moritz still owes me an answer. I don't know how I might be to blame. Now I'd like to ask you whether you know something about the situation [?] in Galicia? With the best regards from your sister, Fanny Fruchter.*

Dearest Friend Hermann.

I, too, will send you a few lines. I am well and have a job. I have no idea where Jacob and my sister might be. Otherwise nothing important. With heartfelt regards, your little girl friend, Cilli. [age ca. 10-11 yrs.].

Letter from Fanny Fruchter to Uncle Harry
(in German)
Hamburg, 24 November 1915

My dear brother Hermann,

I received such a sad letter from you, and want to answer you right away. Believe me, Hermann, I cried no less than you. When I am alone and think about it, my heart bleeds, and I can't believe that I will never see my father and Yossele again.

No, it is too terrible!, but can we overrule God's judgment? Now we all are left alone: totally without parents and without our dear brother. Therefore, dear Hermann, I will see to it that Dora shall come to Hamburg as soon as possible. I will make sure that she will, first of all, learn to write and speak German, and then learn some trade. But first she should settle down nicely. It's not right that she always depends on her brother's money for her living. I will write to him and have Rachel Muhlrad bring the letter over, what, after all, will Aunt Fanny say? She surely will not like to let her go because this is how she gets her money and has [pays?] *a housemaid? I hope that she will first of all open her eyes in Hamburg. I can imagine the situation in which poor Dvora finds herself. I will go this Saturday to the main railroad station and find out how one travels* [from Bolechow to Hamburg?] *nowadays. Tell Morris I ask him to tell Aunt Fanny everything <u>immediately</u>. Should she lack the fare, I will take care of it. Now, my dear brother, I will also* write a card to Max, hopefully he'll answer me. That's all for today. I send you my heartfelt regards and kisses, and hope to receive better news from now on. Also many regards to Sadie, husband and children. And again give my regards to your dear brother Morris. Your ever well-wishing sister Fanny.

My address is: Fanny Fruchter, Grindelberg 55 III, Hamburg. Please tell Morris to keep absolutely secret what I have told him about Cilli Zloczower [probably the accidental loss of one of her eyes]. Since M.'s address was not clear I wrote Yawa [?] instead of Dawa [?], I hope he received the letter. About what Yossele did I have no idea.

Your sister Fanny.

I enclose the card which I want you to <u>return</u>, because it is sacred to me. Many regards also from Cilli and Laura. Maren Waldmann [?] sent a card last week, saying that he was very ill. Sister Fanny.

Postcard from Laura Z. to Uncle Harry
(in German)
Hamburg, 25 January 1916

Dear Brother!

You will forgive me for sending you only a postcard. I know very well that when I write to Moritz [Harry's brother] *you will also be well informed. I am not aware of any other news. I have received your letter and thank you for it. I am glad to know how you are. When I will write to you again, I will also send to you a picture of Chaim. All of us are so far alright, which I hope to hear from you, too. You say that you like ...* [hard to decipher, relates to feelings of nostalgia] *... how things are looking back home. For sure, it's sad, but whoever is alive hopes to live to see better times. However, the people caught up in this present evil war are to be pitied. May God soon send them peace. I can tell you that the day before yesterday Izzie* [Isaac] *has already started school, and the children, Cilli and Sam, are learning well. We now have a nice apartment, large, comfortable and with gas.* [Bundespassage 1/I, Hamburg]. *I have furnished the place pretty well, only I have big expenses. Just the rent alone is already 16 Marks more than others, but that too has to count in with the other expenses. Many heartfelt greetings and kisses from me and my kids. Your wee-wishing sister Laura Zloczower. Chaim is a lazy correspondent. He sends his best regards. Best regards also to your dear brothers and sister, also to my sister-in-law* [Harry's wife, Bessie]. *Cilli* [Chaim's sister] *send you her best regards.*

Postcard from Fanny Fruchter to Uncle Harry (in German) Hamburg, 26 February 1916

Dear Brother Hermann,

I got your letter, but answered it only with a postcard, because Laura told me she had already written to you. I will gladly write again to Bolechow, specifically to Rachel Muhlrad, because I fear Aunt Fanny [sic]. Dear brother Hermann. Since you have invited me to your birthday, I will invite you to mine. Thank you for it.

I will be 21 on ...[?] Adar, according to the Jewish calendar. I can hardly believe it myself. Today I sent Aron Waldman an English dictionary and a novel and I enclosed a small Siddur [prayer book]. Dear Herman, you always ask me to send money to Dvora. That is the least, were it a lot of money I would also have it. I would be very happy if I would hear from her. It is a terrible pity that you have lost .... [?] Tell me how things are with the stepsister Yohebet? Does she live in New York or in Chicago? The questions you have put to me Laura has already answered. I don't know anything more. Oh yes, I still owe you thanks for the nice picture . You do look splendidly. And now, many regards from your good sister, Fanny. Regards to everyone.

Letter from Fanny to Uncle Harry
(in German)
Hamburg, 17 August 1919

Dear Herrmann,

Since I believed I would get mail from you, I drove on empty. It said in the newspaper that mail from America will arrive, and so I enjoyed thinking that I will soon get some sign of life from you, but unfortunately [it didn't come], *so I will be again the one to write first. In May 1917 I sent you as well as Morris each a letter, which were returned to me. I can mail them back again to you at some time. Today I got a letter from Dvora who says that in Bolechow they got a lot of mail from America, but not she. Apparently you have completely forgotten your sister, or what else can I think? This week we got a letter from Nathan* [in Buenos Aires] *which was en route since November 1918. He writes that he will not stay in Argentina in any case, because the country there is very impoverished, and he thinks he might return* [to Germany]. *He also asked whether we have any mail from you, we should send him your address.*

Dear Herrmann, [guess] *what pretty picture I imagine. I picture you or Morris—if he is still single—are making a pleasure trip to us in Hamburg, since no military is in control now and you are free to come without any punishment, and that would be so great, it would be an unending joy. Ach, do surprise us some time. Chaim hasn't worked as a turner for some time: he has a used furniture business. They live at Rentzelstrasse 5 III.* [That was still—in the Grindel neighborhood—where my parents lived till 1929, during the first 5 years of my life.] *Don't you know whether Morris received mail from Aaron, imprisoned in Siberia? We have not heard from him for the past 2 years. Nathan's address is: Buenos Aires. Calle Mexico 3041. Dvora's address: Bolechow at Abraham Halpern. And now, many regards and kisses from your faithful sister Fanny.*

Please do come to Hamburg! Where is Max? Give my regards to Morris and a kiss.

Letter from Fanny to Herrmann
(in German)
Hamburg, 28 October 1919

Dear Brother Herrmann,

I got your letter already a long time ago, unfortunately I had no time at all to answer it before now. Now, my dear brother, why don't you tell me something about your dear wife. I am very curious to know whether you are happy. I wish from my whole heart that you are [happy]. *After all, you are a very good person and you earn it* [to be happy]. *Please write to me more often, it is such a great joy to hear from you. We got along so well in the earlier days. I also had sent you a letter at the beginning of August to your old address in* [name of street illegible(?)] *Did you get that one? I would be happy if I could get a picture of you and of your wife. Regarding Dvora, we already made some efforts to have her come to us, but till now it has always been for naught. Lea Ester had her doctor write a document to the effect that she* [Lea Ester] *is suffering from an illness and absolutely has to have her sister come to care for her. She has sent this document by express* [to Dvora] *and I will wait and see how it works out. I would be very happy if she were here. Now, dear Herrmann, I don't understand at all why I have not heard anything from Morris. Doesn't he have any time for me, or doesn't he want to have any* [time]? *And I don't understand what you are saying: is Morris already in the army? And where is Max serving? Did he fight against us? Here in*

Germany everything looks pretty bad, but you surely read everything in the papers. The cost of everything is sky high. Our currency has no value abroad, and many items are still unavailable. Many people here get from America packages with groceries, as well as clothing and laundry items. I wish I too had a rich uncle there who could make me happy. We have not heard again from Nathan, he was going to get engaged. That Cilli got engaged, I think I have already told you. How is [your] sister Jeoli [?], her husband and children? And how is Lea Branny [?]? I would love to hear from you all the good news. Lea Esther will shortly write to you. I am taking dance lessons, but lead otherwise a very lonely life, since there is nothing to enjoy. The terrible war and the appalling peace wrecked the best years of our youth. If you want to go out, like to the theater or anywhere else, [you'll find] *the last streetcar is running at 9 p.m.* It's no fun to walk in the dark streets. Now, dear brother, take a little time out for me and tell me in a very long letter how things are looking to you.

Many warm regards to you as well as your wife and brothers. Your sister, Fanny.

Letter from Nathan Fruchter (In Yiddish)
Buenos-Aires, 22 August 1922

Dear Brother Hermann!

It is already long ago, long ago, that I have received your letter from you. Unfortunately I soon after lost your address and didn't answer you. I have hear that you got married and have a child, to whom I wish (not knowing her) much luck. From my side I can tell you that I, too, got married half a year ago and, thank God, I'm not doing too badly. I am working in a Jewish newspaper as writer and don't earn a lot, only enough to make a living. I am enclosing a picture of myself and my wife. You surely won't recognize me anymore in the picture, but that's how I look. At the same time I will ask you, dear brother, for a picture of yourself, your wife and children, and write how all of you are doing. Do you see often Morris and Max, and how are they? Give them my regards. Should I get an answer from you, I will see to it that, in future, we will correspond more often and
feel closer from the distance.

With best regards and my regards to your wife and my acquaintances.

Your brother,

Nathan Fruchter

Letter from Fanny Fruchter (in German) Amsterdam, 25 September 1922

Dear Brother Herrman,

Tell me, dear Herrman, why we do not hear from you. You were the only one who would give a sign of life from time to time, and now this too has stopped. Dvora has promised not to forget me, and I see clearly how tightly she keeps her word. It would be much nicer if every 4 weeks one might hear from someone. After all, one doesn't need such enormous time [for it] *and, I think, that much* [time] *we should have left for each other. Don't you think so? Whenever I send you an answer I always write in great detail, but you ... pfui. I really don't find it nice of you. Now, hear this, dear brother Herrman, I returned from Hamburg last week. I went there for a visit to Chaim for 14 days and met an acquaintance, a young man who asked for my hand, which I gladly granted him. Although I have known him already for a couple of years, we have always been like strangers to each other. And now that I have been with him, we got engaged, not officially, but on our word. He is 37 years old and very, very industrious, good, and most of all has a good character. Now I got back to Amsterdam because I have to shop several things and, naturally, I need money for it. My intended, however, should he manage to get an apartment as well as a shop, wants to wait till after Shavuot. To find an apartment is very difficult, and he has to have a shop because he wants to be independent. His occupation is that of an egg sorter* [who shines a light through the egg to sort it], and he gets paid very nicely. But, like I said, he wants to be independent. I am very satisfied with my selection and hope that we will be suited to each other.

How is Dvora, and what is she doing? And how are the conditions [where you are]. Things look pretty bad in Germany, prices are flying sky high not merely every day, but rather every hour. Lea Esther, I'm sorry to say, looks very bad, also her oldest daughter, Cilli. She probably studies too hard. On October 1 she will start her job in an office. To her credit, Lea Esther has some very fine children. How are your wife and daughter? You promised me a picture of them, that I will probably not get any more. Right? When I will get an answer from you, I will write more. I don't hear anything from Morris and Sidy [?] and Max, just as if I don't exist any more.

I'll finish for now.

Many regards and kisses from your sister.

Fanny

Letter from Fanny Fruchter (in German)
Buenos-Aires, 26 July 1932

Dear Brother Harry,

Thank you very much for your dear letter. Well, after I have written to you more than three years ago you are [now] answering it. The address was the right one because it is Nathan's [Fanny's brother]. *He was also surprised to hear from you.*

From Leah Esther in Hamburg I heard that you had told her personally about someone, who knows all of you well, who has gone to Russia. He is a son of Bentlit [?] *Meier. Twelve years ago he was in Hamburg, before he came to America, and he described how bad the situation in North America is. True to say, it is bad all over, you hear that all the time.*

As for me, you know already from my last letter that I got married 3 years ago. Exactly on our anniversary we celebrated the bris of our son, and shortly –please God– I hope to give a little sister as a present to my son, who will have her mother's name. I am enclosing a picture of us, taken 4 months after our wedding, as well as one of our child, age 17 months. As soon as I will get new pictures and I would have the interest [to send them] you will get some.

I'm thinking, if you can imagine it, that I would so like to see you, your wife, also your children, if not in person then at least in a picture. Can't you fulfill my wish? I would also love to see and hear from our other brothers and sisters something personal. Nathan has 2 children, one daughter of 9, and a son, age 6 years. He is an editor of the [Yiddish] press. You probably know about our paper. Leah Esther's oldest daughter [Cilli] got engaged, and will soon get married. Rachel Muhlbad with her children has been here in Buenos-Aires 5 years. Her husband died in the war. The oldest 2 children are married. The daughter has already a child, a little boy, and Shaye is expecting.

In Rachel Maas' family, the oldest daughter is engaged and will get married in a few months. She [Rachel] has 4 daughters. The second oldest who is now already 18 years old, got sick from a terrible fright when she was 2 years old and can _never_ get well. Aby Gottesman's second daughter, Leah—I don't know if you remember her—is already two years here, also engaged and intends to get married beginning September.

How many children does Sadie, or Sara as you call her there, have? Do your children speak Yiddish or only English? If you will answer my letter, I'll write more to you. Heartfelt greetings to you, your dear wife, as well as kisses for your dear children. Please send greeting from me to all, Moritz, Max, Dora and the others.

Fanny Kauf. Write to me at the same address:

Fanny Kauf. Barrio Varela Renan 1250, Buenos-Aires.

Letter from Lea Ester (typed, in German) Hamburg, 24 April 1933

My dear, kind Harry, First I want to tell you that, so that you can read my writing better, I have asked my eldest daughter to type the following lines, and I hope that this won't make you cross.

Before I thank you for your dear letter, I must tell you that you are the best. It came as a big surprise; it also was a great joy, to know that someone, after all, is interested in our welfare. I was even asked by Hende Ruchel of London whether we are still alive. She told me that she had fasted and lit candles in schul when she heard how far the anti-Semitism had gone. God be praised and thanked, we were not very much affected. The boycott [of Jewish businesses] *lasted only one day, everything else in Hamburg remained rather quiet. For the most part all* [Jewish] *newspapers are banned, and what you hear is totally one—sided. Kosher meat is also banned, and so we have no meat .But one thing is clear: we few Jews will now band more closely than before because only sorrow unites. My dear, kind boy, I thank you again for the news about your siblings. I love to hear from all of you and picture you still so young (standing) at the courtyard of your mother and father who was so good to us children. And I then see myself also as young. But all that is figurative, in reality I will soon be a grandmother, since my Cilli who was married last year* [is pregnant] *but lives with us. We had to move to a larger apartment.*

So, dear Harry, you should know that Fanny has two boys and leads a satisfactory marriage. Nathan has a little girl and a boy, but all complain that their financial situation is very bad. Dear Harry, do send me a picture of your wife and children. We all would be very glad. Perhaps your siblings will give us the pleasure to send some pictures of them. You probably know how to make someone happy.

You have perhaps heard that Isaac, we called him Edo, met his death 4 years ago in an auto accident. Simon, who is almost 20 years old, graduated and majored in the chemical field. He is now unemployed. Julius learned to be a furrier, but is unemployed. It is now quite impossible to make a living or do any business. Life is so miserable because young people have no future. Beautiful Germany looks so sad, it was this way all the years since the lost war. What hurts is that things look very different today. To be a Jew and suffer the discrimination is very hard to bear. There is so much we would like to write, but it is better to remain quiet, you surely hear enough [about this] abroad. I fearfully tremble that the business where Sam is employed does not go kaput, because then we can go begging. He gives me as much as he possibly can. The youngest three are still in school. The youngest, Gunther, is a bright boy, a good student. I thank you in the name of the three youngest for the dollar for which I have bought them the things they most needed. And they were very happy with it. My son-in-law is a seaman. He is now on the steamer "Gerolstein" sailing to New York. He has your address and will probably write to you. In any case he will try to find you, if his time and money permit. His name is Sally Schieber.

Dear Harry, don't take it amiss that I write so much. You do want to know it [don't you]. Chaim is no longer well, and I, too, find my work to be heavy. I am very weak, I notice it when I don't have anything left in my bones. And now the loss of jobs makes me despair. But I don't want to make you sad. You brought me joy, and all my 7 children took part in my joy. Therefore, best regards to you and your wife, and let me hear more often from you. Warm regards to your dear children.

Chaim and my children send their best regards. Please give regards to all your siblings.

Your Lea Ester.

Letter from Lea Ester (in German)
Hamburg, 3 November 1937

My dear brother Harry!

It was with great joy that I got your letter of 19 October. I thought it was a dream to get mail from you. Everyone at home, Chaim and the older children, were very happy with it. Naturally, –the letter arrived on Shabbat--you led me back some 35 years to the town of my birth, Bolechow, and I saw you all move in to my house. We, kids, did get along very well, unfortunately we only had the understanding of children. Today, that we have all grown old, it should not be so. Sad to say, America turns everyone into a businessman and not a human being. And that is a big mistake. Anyway, I strayed in my writing. I must thank you warmly, first of all, for your dear words, but I have very much regretted that so many years have passed and while we have such a bad situation, no one wants to know whether we are alive . My thoughts have been with you, children, very often, and I would have loved to know how all of you are doing. But I'm sorry I didn't have any address. Hende Ruchel, do you remember her? Several times she remembered to ask us how we were. I answered her in detail and was grateful that there are still people who do not quickly forget others. Before, dear brother, I answer all your questions, I would beg of you two things which are close to my heart. First, that this letter should not be the last one; that you will one again take the time to write. Second, I would like

Morrie's address. God forbid that I should ask him for something, but I would like to write to him sometime and he should answer me. I also would love to have Lea Brenner's address, but so much all at one time is not to be had. Dear Harry, why haven't you mentioned Mottel, Surcie, Dvora [in your letter]? You say that you are 42 years old, and I am 52, but, after all, we are not old. For sure not in our hearts. I also would love a picture of you, your wife, and your children. Now I will let you know how things are with us.

My husband has been unemployed for three years, which is not exactly news. My oldest daughter, Civvie [Cilli], who has been married for 5 years and has a little girl of 4 yrs is in Trieste [Italy]. Sally, her husband, has gone to sea on a boat plying between Haifa –Palestina– and Trieste. Cilli went there so her husband could be with her and their child every 14 days when the ship was in harbor. They have no bread and are waiting for a certificate that allows them to immigrate to Palestine. My oldest son, Shmuel, is still working in his business, earns well, but must support the house [expenses], as well as Cilli in Trieste. Icic [Edo], a big boy, had a car accident when he was 19 years old which cost him his life. That was 8 years ago. Then there is Simon, who is 24 yrs old, and is enclosing a [his own] letter. He is a sweet, very decent boy with good character and good education. The only thing missing now is any opportunity to make something of himself. Next is Julius, who will be 23 yrs old in January. He got married in Palestine. I also have a *pretty girl, Edith who will be 19 yrs old in January. She is in Tel Aviv, Palestine, at a Wizo School. And here at home I have a girl, Betti who will be 16 years old tomorrow, and a boy Gunther, who made Bar Mitzvah 3 weeks ago. So, if you are smart and can figure everything out in this letter, I would be glad. I also would like to know if Rechel and Meier Aron Schottenfeld are still alive. And where does Percie* [?] *live? In the same town as her parents? Many of my acquaintances have emigrated; each one goes where he can find a good soul that can arrange for him to come. Now I will ask you: Do you remember Cirle* [Cilli], *Chaim's sister. They* [Kistenmacher] *had 2 big shops selling eggs. They did very well, but now it is 2 years that they have lost their business. They have a small apartment and live from their savings. How long can that last? One can die. And he* [Cilli's husband] *is a big and strong young man such a young man who will not be a burden to anyone because he knows the egg business, is very competent, is money minded. He does not shrink from the toughest work, and now he, his wife, one big son age 16 and a girl of 12 are breaking down. It is not so simple for a healthy man, a capable businessman to go about without any employment. He has no one, and Cilli has no one, who could earn the mitzvah to rescue the family from despair by arranging an emigration. People cannot help one another very much, and still there area few among them who think not only of themselves but of others with feeling. So, if you cannot read this letter, let someone read it to you.*

Be well. And warm regards to you, your wife and children.

Your sister, Lea Ester Zloczower

Postcard from Lea Ester (in Yiddish)
Hamburg, 10 January 1938

My dear brother Harry!

I have been waiting so long for an answer to my letter, I cannot understand, my dear brother, what's happening; You yourself have asked about us, and I was so happy you did. I have written to you in great detail and have begged you for an answer, but till today I haven't heard anything. So, my dear brother, don't let me beg you, and answer me, because I have something important to write to you. I would also ask you for Moshe's address. Don't worry, I'm not asking anything from him. I only want to be able to write a letter to him. All I write these days is only to get an answer. Tell me, how is your health? Also send some picture so I can see your wife and children. With heartfelt regards to you and your family from all of us, your sister.

What is your daughter studying? Also my son, who is 13 yrs old, would like to correspond with your son to improve his English. If you have any pictures [of your family] *please send them to me. Don't forget to answer me. Again, my regards to you as well as your family.*

Your sister, Lea Ester Zloczower.

Letter from Laura To Harry (in German)
Hamburg, 9 March 1938

My dearest brother Harry and Family,

I have just received your letter and thank you from my heart. I'm therefore answering you right away because I want to tell you that, although you did not write I had faith in you, and I had hoped that you would still answer me. Well, I was not disappointed. Now my dear Harry, I will answer everything but first I wanted you to know that my son, Simon's biggest wish is to immigrate to America. He is 25 yrs old and the best upbringing. You must look far and wide for someone like him. He is working in a business office. You will never regret it if you would arrange immigration papers for him. He has a good character and knows several languages. To remain in Germany is impossible, and it is my greatest wish to know that the children are in a safe place. That you will understand. My sister [in-law], *Fanny, and Nathan are in Buenos Aires, and they went to some trouble to make it happen* [get immigration papers for Simon], *but nothing became of it.*

If he [Simon] *were a farmer it might be possible to get the immigration papers. And illegally, he would never go. That is our biggest worry: to get the children out of here. Who knows what will happen, he may not be able to get out any more. I want to say again: it will not cost you a cent, and you will have much joy from him because he is cultured* [educated] *and will make a* living for himself. Why didn't you send me the address of Morris? If one only wills it, he will find the time if only to write a few words. I know that my children like me have to make sacrifices for others. It makes me happy that I had the opportunity to do a good deed. I fail to understand how business can top all humanity. Ours is not a small town, everyone is busy with his occupation. But no one forgets his fellow man. America seems to take away all idealism. I'll ask you moreover, dear Harry, to forward the letter to Morris and, if it is not possible for you to do anything for Simon, perhaps Morris will help out. Now my dear brother, my daughter Cilli has been in Trieste already 3 years since the first of May. My son-in-law is a steward with the Bernstein [shipping] line and has sailed from Haifa to Trieste where Cilli had settled. Afterwards they got the certificate, but since my son-in-law is stateless, he needed a "nansen-passport" [for stateless people]. However, the official authorities with their hesitations and delays took so long that they have withdrawn the certificate and promised him another one later. Now 2 years have already passed and he was told that he will get it this summer. Since November '36 the ship Bernstein is laid up, and they wait and wait for months with no income, hoping to get the certificate. They go through a lot, and as much as we can we try to help Cilli, her husband and child. Their situation is very sad. This long time without income kills them. I do not want to write more because it is nothing good.

I have a son in Palestine, who learned well the furrier

trade. He also goes to sea. He is 23 yrs old, married. His ship goes to Haifa and Constanta (Romania), and he gets 4 Pounds monthly with which he little by little furnished his home. Till now his wife also had a job. I still have a daughter who was 19 in January and will graduate from the WIZO school in 4 months. Hopefully she will have luck finding a job since the country is a poor one and one has to struggle hard. She learned infant and childcare. My oldest son, (Sam) Schmiel, will travel to Palestine, God willing, as a tourist for 4 weeks to look around for a job. I'm curious to know how and what he'll achieve, since he will incur a lot of expenses but hopefully it'll pay. My sister-in-law, Cilli Kistenmacher has boy, 16 yrs., and a girl of 12-13 yrs. A few days ago, Kistenmacher left for Buenos Aires with a heavy heart, leaving his family behind.

Ruchel married off a daughter. She has 4 daughters; one died and 2 are with her. Also Hende Ruchel writes from England. She has a married son and one who is not yet married. Her husband left her for another woman. Dear Harry, we are well, thank God, and we live on what Sam and Simon can give us. My apartment is too big for us, now that the kids are gone, but it is not possible for me to sublet because everyone has left the country. It is not possible for me to write to you much, only to express my deepest plea: don't be afraid to help my son, Simon. You will never regret it. If you won't consider me impudent, I will ask you to write to Morris to let Cilli have something, once. It would be a big Mitzvah. She has been in the hospital for the past 3 months, now weighs only 86 pounds and is at the end of her strength. Her address is: Cilli Schieber, Trieste, Via Gaspare, Gozzi 3. If you, dear Harry, think that it would not be comfortable for Morris, or he would not let anyone hear from him, than so be it. I thank you again warmly for your writing and for the enclosure. Keep thinking of us. You are a good person and God will protect you, your dear wife as well as your family protect you from all need and trouble. Be well and with best regards to you and your family, your well-wishing sister, Laura Zloczower.

Please tell me in your next letter where Mottel and Dvora are living. I'm interested to hear from all the children. Doesn't Morris live also in Chicago? Please write soon and confirm at the same time Simon's letter. Special regards also from my husband and our children.

Dear Harry, Simon wanted to enclose a letter, but didn't have the time. Meanwhile I got news from Cilli that she has received the certificate, and this 16th of May all three will be taking off for Palestine. Your sister, Laura.

Letter from Lea Ester (in German)
Hamburg, 1 September 1938

My dear Brother Harry and dear Wife and Children.

You, dear Harry, can hardly imagine the joy, which your affidavit caused. May you all good things that I wish for you come true. Simon wrote to you about other matters, but I hope to God that you will never regret the trouble you went to. Regarding Simon's talents, they will show up, because he will not fail when he has a job and income. I must point out again that he is an educated, neat, and very decent, mature young man, about which you will convince yourself. I am envied here for my well brought up children.

Dear Harry, how come Morrie didn't answer and let's no one hear from him? We, in Germany, thank God that there are Jewish people who are compassionate, have a Jewish heart, and are ready to help and support their Jewish brothers. Otherwise only dear God knows what might happen. My Cilli has been for months in Palestine destitute. If my son-in-law were in America, what a good fortune that would be, because Cilli's husband has been going to sea for over 10 years. He was a steward in first class, also knows several languages and is very handy. A position as a waiter or jobs in several different occupations he could handle well. Also Cilli can take shorthand and type in English. How tormented the children are in Palestine. If Cilli's husband could only get to go on a boat. Julius, my son who is younger than Simon, is also in

Eretz. He passed the examination for being a furrier. But in Palestine there is no need for furs. For the moment, however, he is working on a ship. Well now, I have heard, dear Harry, that Dvora is also in Chicago, and max. Is Max married? And does Dvora have children? It's like this here: I, too, would like to goo to Palestine in spite of the very bad times, since there is nowhere else any opportunity, but the children must have a certain income to apply for our immigration. And then we are 4 persons here. The girl who will be 17 yrs old in two months works in a household, and the boy who will be 14 yrs is still in school. I have no idea how I can ever get out of here. But I am so glad that the children are getting out of here. Please God that Simon will soon find an opportunity for employment. Many, many thanks to you, for all your trouble, also to your dear wife, and your daughter, who makes such sweet effort. Heartfelt thanks and many regards. I would like to know what he [Simon] has to take with him. New items one cannot take abroad, but perhaps a complete featherbed? Perhaps you can give me a clue? Does Lea Breine live in New York? Perhaps you can send me her address. Tell the Committee that it is impossible for you to come up with the [travel] expenses. You will need to help Simon anyway, he should be getting money in Germany because he was born here and is a member of the Jewish community. With many heartfelt regards for you, wife and children,

Your sister, Lea Ester Zloczower

Letter from Laura (in German)
Hamburg, 15 September 1938
(*Reverse side* from Simon—in English)

My very dear brother Harry,

You can hardly imagine what joy and calming it is for us to know that Simon can leave already. Unfortunately it comes at our expense ; the Committee would have paid a part if he would have waited 5-6 weeks longer. He should not do that, because nobody knows what will happen tomorrow, and so we borrowed money wherever we could and sold our dining room to cover the travel expenses. I cannot write all the details, Simon will tell you everything. I only pray to God that he will remain in good health and will find (a job with) a good income. Everything now goes topsy-turvy without any preparations, yet very quickly. In your opinion, dear Harry, it will all be well done, since everything can be straightened out with money, but if things are too late everything will be lost. I will only add that I wish you and your dear family a happy, peaceful New Year. May the almighty credit your ever-so-ready, good deed you did for Simon. With a thousand regards for you, your dear wife and dear children, your ever grateful sister, Laura.

Chaim and, (on behalf of) all my children, send you the same good wishes.

Dear Uncle Harry,

I am very happy to inform you that I have got the visa from the Consul and it happened that I could get a passage, but only tourist class (instead of 3rd class). I shall travel per S.S."Manhattan" (United States Line) which arrives at New York on the 29th of this month 9 o'clock in the morning. Immediately on my arrival I shall phone or write to you. I want to stay in New York about 8-10 days and my first address is there with my acquaintances:

S. Zloczower
c/o Gumprecht
600 141st Street
New York City

If you can write to above address and state any good friend or relative where I can live for a few days, this would be a great help to me. Ma thinks that Aunt Lea Braine is living there and how is their residence?

As no mail will reach me still in Hamburg, please write to New York or perhaps you will bee there (but <u>do not</u> travel for myself only). Many, many thanks again and you will hear from [me] in due course.

Best regards to all, your nephew Simon.

Letter from Mutti to Uncle Harry
(in German)
Zbaszyn, 12 February 1939

My dear brother Harry, Wife and Children,

I received your dear letter, as well as Simon's, for which I thank you for your trouble and your kind lines. My dear Harry, you and your dear wife don't realize what mitzvah you have earned by giving Simon the opportunity to get out of Germany. I believe I will be grateful to you all my life long. Now I will answer all your questions. First of all, we have not heard anything from Warsaw, perhaps some message will come in a few days, because Chaim wrote (from Warsaw?) that he would like to have the affidavits already in his hands. He wants to have photocopies made of them and then send a copy to Sam in England. At any rate, from there everything will be processed more quickly, and we could possibly wait out our time there (in Warsaw). In Poland everything is probably much cheaper, but the hate of Jews leads every day to fights with Jews in spite of the police ban. I'll tell you a little incident so you can get the picture. We had to go register and, since we are Z (last in the alphabetical order) it happened that we got to register only just before 10:00 p.m. when it closes. The people (registrants) here crawl, they are so slow; it took 3 weeks to get the registration done (presumably because it took that long to get through the alphabet). When Chaim was on his way home two guys approached him and hit him on the head. Thank God, it was not very bad. His hat flew off. He was not prepared for such a thing and moreover he was tired from standing around all day. He came home all broken up after a half hour in the wind and the rain. This is what happens to many here; some make reports, but who knows who those hooligans are? In this respect, things here are more horrible than in Germany, because the people here consider these (fights with Jews) to be commonplace. I thank you and your kind wife again for the love you are showing to Simon. Simon tells me everything in detail, also about his income. The best thing is that I can easily believe him and what he writes is true. I can understand that Morris has no time, but thousands of people found out today that one dare not miss the time to help, if one can do so. [This seems to imply that a lot of Jews have discovered that they have "missed the boat".] *If you should see Morris, please tell him that he will never regret his help and that all of us will be deeply grateful. My Betti s a pretty girl and has been a household help already for the past 2 years. I hope she will easily be able to take care of herself and not be a burden to anyone, if only the time for it had come (so she could show how mature she is). The HIAS or the Committee (some help agency) is not helpful at all; when everything is ready and has been arranged, then one can (be helped to) go. No one among us refugees got to go to Warsaw, since we were not permitted to leave Zbaszyn. Whoever has a lot of pull has it easier and better, that's the way in the whole world. For today I will end (this letter) with many heartfelt regards for you and your dear wife who is like an angel* to Simon. Heartfelt regards for your dear children from Chaim, Betti, Gunther, and me.

Your well-wishing sister, Lorcie.

Postcard from Mother and Others (in German)
Lwow, 26 July 1939

My beloved child, Guntherl!

I received your dear card as well as the one from Family Schneider. We all thank you from our heart. Thank God you arrived safely [in "Centos" Otwock], *everything else will work out. Tell me whether you need some pocket money or a packet with cookies. Just today I'm writing to Simon; yesterday I got a letter from him. If your stay there is really going to take some time, send Sam a postcard right away and let him know. How was your arrival there? Getting to the address, did you reach a Kontor* [?]*? You were in a sad mood* [when leaving for Warsaw], *which was very painful for me, but it is after all for your best. Take care that you stay healthy, eat and drink. I will be glad to send you some money if you can buy yourself something. How many children are there* [with you]*? If something important happens, I will let you know. I have pretty much organized everything. Today I am doing the laundry. I send you my kisses and best regards. I am thinking of you always. Mama.*

Best regards, and stay upbeat. Papa.

Greetings, and hoping to see you again soon, Betti. Write before you sail to England, so I can enclose a letter for Isi.

G...H!... The meaning of these two letters —later—. Now I want to send you heartfelt greetings, wish you all the best, and thank you for your nice and dear words, which gave us great joy. May all go well for you, and all your starts in life be accompanied with good luck. Your Munio, Julie, Lusie [?], and Sol [?]

Letter from Mutti (& Betti) in German Lwow, 2 August 1939

My sweet child, Guntherl,

We received both cards today. I am so sorry [to hear about] *your itching. This lovely land gives you the cup of bitterness filled to the brim to drink. But, thank God, help comes nearer every day and every hour. As far as money is concerned, don't worry. I only want you to have something to snack on, fruit or cream, sweets. It is very hot, so dress as lightly as possible, and wash up several times a day. Dear Guntherl, write at once to Sam the same what you have written us, regarding a haircut in Gdynia. Perhaps it is possible for him to write* [to someone] *to prevent it. He should explain that you have been well cared for at home and that you are quite particular* [about your hair]. *You could get sick about it for weeks. They should treat your hair just like the girls', they can't after all cut off all the girls' hair. When children in Germany were sent* [to a health camp] *with bugs in their hair to recuperate, their hair was also cut short. Hair grows back in. Whatever, do what is possible and write to Sam about everything. Above all else, don't worry. The main thing is, stay healthy, don't get upset, eat, drink, and buy whatever you have a taste for. Ask where you are what you can do for the stabbing pains, or ask in a drug store whether they have something that's effective. Yesterday I got a letter from Anny Teitelbaum, she is still in Zbaszyn. Also* [a letter] *from*

Simon with playing cards. I can expect to get a picture from him soon.

He copied the speech he gave at Harvey's Bar Mitzvah and the one Harvey himself gave. Also, he advised me, although it doesn't look like a war is coming to go into the interior [of Soviet occupied Poland or the U.S.S.R.]. With us personally, there is nothing new. Hopefully we'll soon get some mail from Eretz. Are you the whole day in your room? Have you lost too much weight? With us nothing is happening. We are looking every day to see whether we have mail. On Friday I will write to you again. I enclose a postage stamp. Do you have something to read? Betti would like to chat with you a little. Be well and may we hear from you many good things that we can share.

Many regards and kisses, Mutti.

Dear Gunther,
When I read your card and I came to your itching, you can compete with me (but kindly let it be), and neither should you regard my business as "shitvesdig" [as a partnership with you], I had to laugh loud, although I felt very sorry for you. Since we have been in "Poilen" [Poland] we want the many different insects (bug, flea, etc.) keep up our connection, as they go from me to you and visa versa. Now something else. Absolutely don't let them cut your hair in Gdynia.

Let them, first of all, check your hair thoroughly. If you don't have any lice (you must brush your hair well *every day) then you rightfully should keep your hair. If you do* [have lice] *then they should wash your hair (with vinegar) in Gdynia, etc. They are not going to cut Selma H.'s full, curly hair either, possibly they might only wash it out. When you are in Gdynia go to the end of the line of boys so that they won't rebel when they made an exception with you. Don't tell anyone your intentions and write to Sam in detail. He might possibly be able to help. He should write immediately to Gdynia because the mail takes a long time to get to England. And how are things with your ruggelech? How long did they last? Is the wine also finished? Did you get from your new comrades German books to read? I have packed away, ready for the trip, my dictionary and cannot therefore get to it. Does "relations"* [the English word] *mean related? Mama acquired a Primus* [portable burner, for cooking] *which burns well and economically. Is there any news where you are? Hopefully there won't be any war any time soon, because then I couldn't even think of getting to England. I still have one more request to make of you. I don't want him to get anything from me in writing, only my greetings that you will forward to him. Please ask him, or try to find out, why he writes to me so seldom. Let me know when you will be in London. Perhaps he has no money, desire, or patience for corresponding, perhaps his parents have forbidden it. I would very much like to know the exact reason. Please don't forget it. I rely on you and send you regards from your most flea-bitten relief-seeking sister, Betti*

My Guntherle!

Unfortunately you will have to bear with the next couple of days. When you get to England you will hopefully be able to do as you want. With heartfelt greetings, Papa. [Betti adds the words "from your Pius" in front of Papa's signature.]

[from Betti] *P. S. What beautiful things did you see in Otwock, other than fleas or lice?*

Postcard from Mother and Others
Lwow, 4 August 1939

My beloved boy!

We got your dear card, also mail from Sam and a copy of what he had written you. Dear child, with us there is nothing new. My worry is that I have not heard anything from Palestine till today. Betti wrote again to the Committee in Warsaw at Sam's urging. Dear child, if you have any money left over, send it directly to Schneider so they can draw it [from the bank] *themselves. Most of all be careful with money and with the books which should be in a locked suitcase. Treat yourself to whatever your little heart desires, snack and enjoy. The man who came to papa before you left, went to Krakow where he was robbed. Herr Bleich is now in Hamburg. Love and kisses. Mama.*

M.G.H. Don't ever think that I'm calling you: Mussolini, Goring, or even Hitler. May they drop dead and their death be our redemption. I mean simply: "My Good Hallodrie [an endearing, made-up name]. *Wish you all the best. More next time. Munio.*

This time only greetings. Don't itch so much! Save this card for your collection. May we soon see each other. B.

Letter from Mutti (in German)
Lwow, 6 August 1939

My beloved boy, Guntherl!

Yesterday morning came a registered letter. You handled that cleverly and correctly, since you don't really know what upset you saved yourself by sending it quickly. When I read your sad, almost despairing letter, I immediately wrote to Sam, enclosed your letter, urged him to not to pass up whatever might help, and quickly sent off the letter per express. As I figure it, Sam would get the letter Monday, the 7th or Tuesday the 8th. Perhaps he can get something done at the Committee that you can come [with the others] *on the 11th. Sam will, at any rate, do everything possible. About that I have no doubt, and you can rest assured. But my beloved child, that different things plague you, like the itching, or perhaps during your sleep or while eating, you must not take so much to heart. Think of the itching, which probably is one that makes you most nervous, as an illness which will soon get better with God's help. Regarding your eating, in so far as possible substitute* [what you don't eat] *with snacks. I will send you money if you need it. Regarding your clothing, wear what you like, the best thing would be the linen pants. Everything will be washed and sorted out in London, since everything is washable. Enjoy all you can. Think how many think of you lovingly and are ready to help you. Regarding the hair cutting, that is the way they do it in the military; the proudest heads of the richest, well groomed have their hair cut so short just like the lice-ridden street urchin. But that grows back in, it's no reason to lose your head over it. What is your great despair all about? If only I knew, I could perhaps ease it. Many people would be* [willing to be] *in prison for half a year if they could only know that their frightful life will get better and that they are heading toward a* [better] *future. When I complain to someone about how I am hurting for you, they laugh at me, because they have bigger problems and would readily exchange places with you. I noticed this Shabbat Jewish boys standing in the street and I looked at them and could have wept, and they even have a home and live with their parents. Don't let yourself get weak and hung up on sad thoughts, because it depresses you and ruins your health. You must maintain a good mood, otherwise life has no value. Do you know the saying "Laugh, Bayazzo?" No matter how much it hurts, show the other side. I hope that Sam's study books will give you some distraction,* [I hope] *also that you will now make the 8 August departure. Don't load yourself down in advance with worries, wait, and much good happens unexpectedly. I will write you again tomorrow or the day after.*

Letter from Betti (in German)
Lwow, 8 August 1939

Dear Gunther!

We received this morning your postcard. Many thanks. It is a pity that you are not leaving [with the transport] *on the 11th this month, but you will surely leave on the 25th. If only some but not all will be leaving, you will be for sure among those who are leaving. Sam would not tolerate another postponement, he will fight for you to leave* [for London] *on the 25th of this month. Let it be a consolation to you. We don't wish to see you in Lwow. Better in London. And now you do not need to be proud only of Sam, but also of Uncle Munio. As you know, he wrote many, many poems and theater plays (only in Yiddish) that were printed. The day before yesterday Uncle Munio read to us some pieces from his works, which were fantastic. The he showed us a big clipping from a newspaper with the following caption: A Wedding Prank, a Jewish Theater Play, written by M. Schneider, Lwow. Uncle Munio created it and had it already staged some time ago. It had played also in Zbaszyn, which had a most enthusiastic audience. These lines come from that piece: shildik in dem is nor mayn nos* [only my nose is to blame for this] *and Gevalt vos vil mayn nos fin mir* [Help! What does my nose want from me]. *Please tell it to Selma H. Now you can at least boast about your uncle. Yesterday we were at the Committee. If we will have achieved anything, we will let you know. There* [at the Committee] *we met a young man who with his father was sitting next to us on the train from Zbaszyn to Lwow. He told* [his story] *in front of everybody. He had stayed in a super-grand house with servants. But there were bedbugs, so he moved out. Now he lives in a room where there are not only bedbugs but also fleas. He showed the people* [in the train car] *the bites on his body, cursed Lemberdreck* [dirty Lwow] *and broke into song: Gevalt, vos vellen fleas un bugs fin mir. Gevalt in all dos ohn a shir* [A variation of the earlier verse].

We all laughed. Got some mail today from Fraulein Fiebelman. She writes that she doesn't know when she will go to Eretz. It seems everything is getting stuck. Since the transport from Ellguth, that she is on, would go illegally to Eretz [this is written in Hebrew to avoid the censor], *it costs a lot of money, which they don't have. Besides, she already has a permit* [to enter England] *for a housekeeper's job, 100 km from Ireland. She doesn't know: should she now go to England on Hachsharah* [a preparatory camp for immigration to Palestine], *when she doesn't even understand the language of the land* [Hebrew], *besides she would have gone to the German Hachsharah for nothing. Or should she wait in Germany for her move to Eretz? But what if, God forbid, a war breaks out soon? Furthermore, she wrote that the Echernforder Hospital was turned into the Friedrichbergs Mental Hospital. The patients are in the Carolinen Strasse, the same with the students* [boys and girls] *from the T.T.R.* [Talmud Torah Real Schule]. *Since there aren't many left in Hamburg, all find a place in the Carolinen school. T.T.R. became a camping ground for Nazis, and the Born Street Synagogue is already completely demolished. I got a letter also from Isi. Since, with God's help, you will be able to see him yourself, I don't need to write about him to you. He moved, and his new address is: Isi Sabielak, London E.2. Bethnel Green Road 98, England. Since he doesn't have your address and Sam, too, wants to move, Isi cannot come to see you, would you go to see him?*

[Mutti added]

Betti's cough is unchanged. As soon as I get mail from Israel I'll write. Got a letter from Aunt Fanny, but nothing that might interest you. I must go to the dentist. I lost a tooth ____[?] and it looks bad. Betti, too, has to get a filling.

Letter from Sam to the Whole Family
(in German)
London, 8 August 1939

Dear Parents, Dear Betti!

Many thanks for your express letter of the 5th inst. ["inst." means the "instant" or current, month; i.e., August], *which I received only today because of the local holidays. The enclosed letter from Gunther of the 3rd inst. I am returning to you herewith. The copy of Betti's letter to the Committee in Warsaw I will keep, since it was meant for me. The letter* [Betti's] *was written correctly. Please inform me at once of any response* [to that letter]. *I find it peculiar that Chassel* [someone with a connection] *has not written to me yet, although he promised to be helpful to me because of his connection to the once Betti submitted the "reports" to the local Committee for the acquisition of household-permits. If I don't hear from him soon, I'll complain to him again.*

Immediately after I received your letter I went to the local Committee to inquire about his case. Based on the information I obtained, I see absolutely no reason to worry. It is true that Gunther could not have been scheduled to join on the transport here on the 28th ult., and that the date of the departure of the remaining Otwock-children was postponed from the 11th to the 25th inst. That was due to internal reasons. It is now absolutely sure that the children will come here by boat from Gdynia on the 25th inst. The voyage will start on a Friday, and the children will arrive in London only on Wednesday, the 30th inst. This is because the ship will skirt Sweden and not traverse the Kiel Canal to avoid touching the German coast. [A very wise move.] Gunther will then continue [his trip] *from here to Cardiff where a family has guaranteed to foster him. I will accompany him there.* [I don't recall that he did.] The local Committee told me that one could say his placement is a stroke of luck because he will be unusually well cared for. I will personally take charge of all details in Gunther's case, so that you won't have to worry. Even if he should remain at first in Cardiff, I will keep up my contact with him. I will visit him occasionally, or he will visit me, and I will always see to it that he is doing well. It is preferable that Gunther goes to Cardiff (instead of possibly remaining with me in London), since he will be with a seemingly well-situated family. The people can easily provide for his board and lodgings, and more importantly, for his immediate future (education and study). They can do this far better and sooner than we, in London, could with our modest means at this time. Gunther always has the option later on to come to me in London, when we should consider it the right thing. His experiences in Cardiff will be important, contributing factors in the decision.

In any case we will deal with this problem again when all of you will be here insofar as a final decision has not been made. As you know, we here have been making efforts to find an apartment. The rentals are, however, so high that we have so far not been able make any decision, even though the cost for our storing our furniture, for the past 6 months, has been going up steadily. Luckily, we have now found something that seems to come up to our expectations in every respect. Last week we had a talk with the owner, and we should hear tomorrow whether he is ready to meet our requirements regarding the décor (papering, painting, etc.). The apartment is only a ½ hour from the city; it has 4 rooms and 2 halls (which can be turned into 2 rooms), central heating as well as running hot and cold water. The house is on a lovely, quiet side street, without shops or traffic. It has a wonderful, park-like garden in the back and a small garden in front, which the janitor takes care of. There are 2 other residents in our two level house. Our apartment is on the 1st floor. Good shopping areas, bus and train stations can be reached in 5 minutes by foot. Well, in every respect idyllic. Hopefully, all will go well. The rent is £ 100 p.a., circa £ 8½ a month, which, based on local conditions, is at least 30-40% cheaper than it would be ordinarily.

My work still suffers somewhat from the fact that I haven't had till now a real home. I have to work a lot at home. In the crowded conditions of the corridor-apartments this was only possible with great difficulty. That should soon change, hopefully.

Dear Mama! I am terribly sorry that you are so worried. I hope that also your situation will soon turn for the better. What I'll then be able to do I will do any time, as you know, because I wish very much that you, as well as Papa and the children would be here. It is regrettable that we have not heard anything from Cilli about herself. After all, she has given us cause to worry about her since she gave birth. It would be lovely if she would now, as before, give us running accounts of how she and all the family members there are doing. In many instances postcards would suffice because it would save postage. For now you will get from me the enclosed letter from Cilli of 2nd inst. that was addressed to me —since I don't know whether Cilli wrote to you directly--, together with 2 cute pictures (one of Inge, one of Cilli, Sally, and Inge) which I also received today. You can keep the letter and the pictures because I do not need them any more to answer Cilli. – Also many thanks for your warm wishes. I think Edith and I will be ready to get married in 1-2 months. How much would I give to have you here then!

Dear Gunther!
You can discern from the above lines the matters that concern you. Be confident and hang in there bravely for this short time. You have gone through much more and are after all an up and coming young man. That involves responsibilities. In just 2-3 weeks I'll perhaps be able to shake your hand. Regarding your letter to Lemberg, of 3rd inst.: You did right sending the 10 Shillings to Lwow, given the depicted circumstances. You can get occasionally from there small amounts, which I cannot send you from here because small bills [Polish money] are here not available. As a matter of fact, I think nobody needs to worry unnecessarily

about all of you getting your haircut. This procedure is not a punishment, but only a measure to prevent vermin getting into your hair, it is necessary and in your common interest. The hair will soon grow back in again and, after all, we still have summer that makes a shorn head in this respect quite tolerable. [The information that] *a part of the children will sail on the 11th inst. is incorrect. I learned from a reliable source—from the local caseworker of the Committee—that <u>all</u> will start together the journey on 25th inst. In any case, you are among those on the 25th inst. I hope you can now sound more confident and with inner calm in your letters to Lwow so that they do not have to suffer even more than they necessarily have to. Think of the predictable affect every letter you write has on the recipient. You are otherwise such a thoughtful and considerate boy.*

If Gunther needs some clothes (he writes about a torn pair of pants) it may then be perhaps possible for you to send him a replacement. We here have to keep all expense down as far as possible because the people in Cardiff will surely do more, very gladly and without any sacrifice than we can, given our major retrenching. If necessary, I'll get Gunther the things he needs right here. Consider it lucky that you, dear Gunther, are cut off from the outside world. If you were to read the daily newspapers, you would get more disturbed than the present situation objectively calls for. It is serious, all right, but I don't believe one should really count on warfare for the immediate future. Therefore it is much better that one spares himself the anxiety which would seize you, whether you want to or not, if you read the constant lectures of the daily papers. Trust your lucky star. You, too, will have better days. Busy yourself as much as you can with the English language. Write to me often, perhaps per postcard, and confirm the receipt of the textbooks. –

In your letter to me of 4th inst. you write about negotiations in Warsaw with Kaiser (the secretary of the local Committee) that are pending. I talked today with Kaiser and he confirmed that the transport of all children will proceed on 25th inst. By the way, he told me he also met you (or, only saw you?). Don't worry about your friend, Rudi Kleinbrodt. I received today the confirmation from the local Committee that he like will find himself likewise among that circle of children who will leave Poland for England on 25th inst. Enclosed is his picture, which you had asked me to return.

Dear Cilli!
Many thanks for your letter of 2nd inst. We were really very worried about you, and I am glad that you have meantime overcome the after-effects of giving birth. I waited so long to get at least a postcard from you that would tell me how the birth of the child went and how its progress is going. Well, thank God that you can now put us at ease. I wish you and Ruth all the best, health, good luck, and a balanced disposition since, as the second born, she should have been a boy. But that, too, is all to the good. I am sending you as a token £ 2:10:-. from which you can perhaps let her have

something from her uncle as a birthday present. Because I want to send Lulu [Julius] and Tamara [Irma] £1:10:- and Edith £1 (for the pattern), I am sending you by the same way, like last time, £5. Please distribute the money accordingly. I haven't heard from Lulu for a long time how he is doing economically. In any case he will buy himself a little something for the small amount and be able to get Tamara a small surprise. In any case he will buy himself a little something for the small amount and be able to get Tamara a small surprise. By the way, I cannot say much today about my local efforts and myself because the letter would be too long. For now I have to answer the letters I have received. At the next opportunity I will tell you more about myself. Be so good, dear Cilli, to let Lulu read your copy of this letter, and then send it to Simon because I cannot make more copies. Both are equally interested in the content of this letter, even more so since they, like you, have not heard much from me lately. Only with Lemberg do I correspond regularly.

Back to the first and most important question in your letter of 2nd inst. It is about Gunther who, as you had mentioned, received the promise of a certificate, and would have to arrive in Eretz by 30th September, if indeed he wants to make use of it. First of all I want to say that you know my Jewish Weltanschauung. I am a Zionist and have not changed in any way because of the recent events. If I am not going now the way I had hoped to go, it is due to circumstances that were more powerful than any of our voluntary decisions. *All of us who left Germany did so under absolutely involuntary concomitant conditions. The force of events led us to decisions and directions that were not (or, better yet: not) anticipated. If I were in Eretz, after calm preparations, at a time of normal events, I would be forced* at once *to look for a new place and an environment where I could function,* [which might have been an option] *when I was expelled from Germany at the end of last year along with other Poles. I had to find this new environment not just for me, but more fundamentally for our parents and siblings so as to strengthen them right now and to facilitate the continuation of their journey from their asylum to a final land of immigration. I am glad that I have succeeded actually to contribute a little, and I hope to cope* [successfully] *with the task sooner or later. I cannot see now if it will be possible for me then to carry out my own plan and go to Eretz, because I would first have to get our dear parents and Betti as well as Gunther settled, which can only be done here. Only* then *can I evaluate the situation.* (depending on how things have meanwhile developed) *and make further decisions for myself.*

After this thoughtful digression, back to the topic. My orientation as a Zionist has not changed in any way. And I believe Gunther's basic orientation tends to go in the same direction. I must mention that I nevertheless am coming to the conviction that it is better for Gunther not to go to Eretz for the time being. *It may be more possible for him in a few years. Now, however, questions of the present and for the immediate future need to be decided. It seems to me absolutely necessary to provide him, while we still can, with the preconditions for his further education and promising, successful studies, since the coming years will be the basis for Gunther's professional development and, at the same time, be decisive for his future way of life. Working in his profession he will show what he is capable of. His profession should also afford him the possibility of living an appropriate existence, since he has to apply all his strength to achieve something and become a man. We need to find for him a suitable selection of occupations and, by means of setting him on the right path, provide him with a springboard.*

There is hardly any doubt whatever where Gunther can have a better education, and where he would have better possibilities opening up after the end of his studies. In any case, in London! Gunther's guarantor, the local committee, and I will continue to try to help him along on his way. The further question—Eretz or another country—Gunther will be able to decide after he finishes his studies, and if not, we will all be ready and glad to make the decision easier for him. I can see in your letter that you were thinking the same. I therefore suggest that you send the certificate to Mama's address so that (just in case) she would have it in her hands. When Gunther will be in London she will send it on to me. In any case, no Polish relief organizations should know any part of this, lest Gunther's departure [from Otwock] *be jeopardized. Therefore you and our dear parents must be extra vigilant in this regard! Things are different for Betti although I believe that she, too, can get a good education here (in social work). We will see what can be done here when she hopefully arrives here in 2-3 weeks. Is there also a prospect of Betti getting a certificate? Regarding your question whether I still support our dear parents, I beg you, don't have any worries about it. I am in constant contact with them and, as far as my means and possibilities permit, they will always get* [from me] *what they need. How I support her is less of a worry for me; it is a fact that Mama doesn't allow herself anything, and in a hurtful* [self-abasing?] *way is very economical (only in her mind she is afraid she might be too demanding). That leads to their living under undignified conditions and, what I fear but do not actually know, to their insufficient food. I would always consider such conduct wrong because it is more damaging than useful, and I hope that Mama allows herself, little by little, more than she has so far. I will send back to you, dear Cilli, the pictures I have asked for (Inge in the kindergarten) as soon as I receive them, at least after my move, which will hopefully take place in 14 days.*

Dear Edith!
I have a bad conscience also in regard to you. You have not seen any line [of writing] *from me for a long time, although I have acknowledged by postcard receipt of the bast-pattern. I hope that the £1, which Cilli will give you in my name, will cover your costs for it. Please list again precisely the cost for all Bast-pieces and wood works; it would be best for each piece, "free*

London," (that is, postage included but not duty). If possible, don't show the prices in Polish money but in English money, and note the discounts for 50, 100, or more pieces of the particular object in percentages. I am honestly sorry that, however important this matter may be for you, I cannot deal with this matter at this time. I have had too many immediate problems to look quietly after the marketing of your products. Some of my worries have, thank God, been settled (I want to mention that I must still hold off a detailed letter about me). And when we will have moved into our new apartment (by then I will possibly have your answer) I will have more time and quiet to deal with your questions, which I will naturally do gladly and conscientiously. I am particularly sorry that I have not been able so far to please Shmuel, whom I thank for his recent addition to a letter, but he may be sure that I will do everything within my power to comply with your wishes. What is really your own work [on the products]? Or do you buy the best pieces as well as the wood objects ready made? It would be best if you would quote at the same time your cost —naturally in total confidence—so that I can judge myself in case of a possible offer whether you would still be interested or not. The detour via Eretz—aside from the postage—costs a lot of time. Could you perhaps find out who the exporter there is of these articles, and who is the receiver here. On my part I will try to find out, in 2-3 weeks at the earliest, what merchants are paying here for such things and what the resale prices are.

Regarding our dear parents you wrote in your letter of 9th July, which strangely arrived only on the 5th inst., that they had better go to the interior of Poland. You would know that this has happened meanwhile. What you perhaps don't know is that they have been living there, 4 persons in <u>one</u> room until Gunther went to Warsaw (hence to Otwock), with all the luggage that got sent to them from Germany and what they brought with them from Zbaszyn. [You may not know…] that they have neither electricity nor gas in their and room, and equally lacking in any additional space for kitchen facilities or storage. It got now a little better because there is more space since Gunther left (unfortunately it also caused Mama much pain). It will be a little improvement when Betti comes here. Nevertheless the conditions there are terrible, and I hope to have our dear parents here before long.

I will get around to do something about the brown necklace. Does it really have to be brown? There are such nice small wooden blocks in red, also patterned in red-white. You like something appealing. It would have been good if you had told me for what occasion you want the necklace. I could have considered the purpose of the necklace [when looking] *at the selection. Please send me perhaps a postcard to make it clear.*

My Dear Ones! Don't be cross with me if I have not written to everyone this time. I will catch up next time. Also, warmest regards to all of you,
Your Sam.

Letter from Mutti and Betti (in German) Lwow, 21 August 1939

My dearest child, Guntherl!

Today I received your dear letter of 19 August. We are happy, as usual, to see your dear handwriting, and thank God that you are finally getting close to your goal. May your way be blessed with good fortune, joy, and good health. May we share your good times. I strongly hope to God that you may also have much good luck, because you got not only a permit [US affidavit?] *but also at the same time a Certificate* [for Israel], *which we have to decline. Now, my dear boy, I doubt whether you told me the truth about your appetite and health. But God will help. I will tell you something about your pants; I paid dearly for my stupidity. First, I spent over 5 Zloty for the sewing and materials. Then he* [the tailor] *stitched the faded pieces willy-nilly together, and you couldn't possibly wear the pants. And so, Papa took the pants to be dyed. Early this morning I went to get them and paid an additional 2.20 Zloty, and made my second mistake: I paid before I took a good look. The stains were still there, only brown and not in their original grey-green. Now I don't' want to send you this rag, because you are not going to wear it. I will make a local boy happy with it, in exchange for redeeming the good wishes. It was such a shame, but we are used to shame* [misery]. *For example, I am missing Betti's slippers, which I bought her in Zbaszyn and packed in the bed bag. Papa's grey summer coat is missing. I don't know where that disappeared, etc. I see I have to pay tuition* [for learning from mistakes] *and feel bad that you have to suffer for it, since I intended to send you with the pants a sweet good-bye gift. Now that I am not sending you the pants, sweets being expensive, it doesn't pay* [any more]. *Besides, it may come too late. Again, everything will be thrown out.*

My dear boy! I hope you have a good voyage. May dear God grant you the wonderful meals they have on board, make good use of it, and enjoy. You will probably not get [any more in Otwock] *any mail from us, because it will take three dates before we will know your departure date. And so I say a heartfelt farewell to you. May things go as well for you as I am hoping for. May we see you again under more fortunate circumstances. Amen. You will then write to me in great detail, and I will forward it to Eretz and perhaps from there to Chicago, so that the postage won't cost too much. You will also need to economize with the postage. Again, much, much good luck on your new journey through life. Amen. Mutti. Please look always carefully after your things, so you won't miss anything.* [Once you miss something] *it is then too late. We are waiting for mail from you and, after your arrival* [with the new address on the letter] *you will hear from us. Be neat so that the people will like you.*

[From Betti]

Dear Gunther! First of all I want to draw something to your attention. We didn't let Uncle Munio see the last cards you sent, because you wrote many regards to <u>Family Schneider</u> [sic]. Uncle Munio felt very offended. To acquaintances, like Lewowie, Blitzowie et cet. [made-up names] you can send greetings for the <u>Family</u>, because they are strangers with whom you are only acquainted. Uncle Munio is your uncle, a blood relative, and you don't give him the customary title. He feels, therefore, on a par with a stranger. Please don't spare your words and write soon to <u>Uncle</u> Munio, <u>Aunt</u> Julia. et cet. They also care about your welfare, are interested in you, and are even proud to have a nephew who at his age is so intellectually advanced. Now another thing. A short time ago I joined a religious club, like Mizrachi. About 6 girls are in this group. They immediately welcomed me so lovingly as can only be the case with fanatics. Only two [of them] understand Yiddish, the others, tylko popolsku [only Polish]. I believe I now know Polish a little better than you, and pisac [writing] as well. Girls of my age from the group went up the Zamek (mountain). [There must have been more who climbed up.] At one point something broke and many girls fell off the mountain onto the street below. I think 8 died and 5 were wounded. What a crying shame. I am taking a closer look at this club to remember it clearly when I'm abroad. I now have a request for you. I have no patience to write to Isi. I could not possibly tell him that the fleas won't leave me in peace and that I *always have to go on a flea hunt. I have already caught two and have murdered them with the red hand of Mafia. He does not know the little mouse trap in which we live, nor that we have to go down two streets to fetch clean water. He does not know either anything about the thieves. (Their finger dexterity is so skilled that they can unbutton a man's jacket and vest undetected.) They cut Papa's watch chain while he was <u>walking</u> and stole the watch that was then loose from the pocket. Papa noticed a weak tug (in his vest) and instinctively felt for his watch. Papa grabbed the man next to him, threatened to make a scene and a scandal if he doesn't get his watch back immediately. After a long back and forth Papa got his watch back but had to buy a new chain. Please do me a favor. When you will be at Isi's give him my most heartfelt greetings, and tell him everything; from our arrest in Hamburg till now. Tell him about the bug and flea infested Lemberger garbage, and about the half-crazed children in Otwock. Don't leave anything out. On my behalf, tell him everything. OK? From our window, ca. 150 meters from us across the meadow, I could see very clearly on a hot and windy day a fire burning. If the wind had blown our way it might have been dangerous for us. A boy, out to smoke a cigar but afraid of his father, went into the shed. Since he was not careful, everything was soon aflame. The fire burned down <u>six</u> houses. Small ones. The fire brigade arrived, crawling, at the end. Four fire trucks. There was no water in the whole street. There was one hydrant two streets farther up, but because of the considerable distance from the fire, the fire truck could* *lay only one hose. To fight 6 little homes with only one water hose!! Dogs and horses were released from their stalls and ran like crazy again and again back into the fire. They said there were also cows. They couldn't release them quickly enough from their iron chains. As 4 men pulled a cow to one side, the cow pulled in the other direction. It was a sad picture to watch. The people, who are so terribly poor, living in such squalor, are now homeless. I saw everything as if it were a movie. Do you know the difference between the Hamburg fire department and Lwow's? Gunther, make sure that you have <u>all</u> your things with you when you leave. Don't leave anything in Otwock! If you still have a few groschen left, buy some sweets for yourself. You can't use any Polish money on the boat. How many children scheduled to go to England are left in Otwock? Selma H. also? To what address shall we now write to you? Many regards and all the best. May everything turn out the way you wished.*

Your sister, Betti.

Postcard from Mutti (in German)
Lwow, 28 January 1940

My Dear Boy,

Should you get this card as we got yours, [it should tell you that] *we are all well. Dearest boy, Gunther. Write again and let us know about your health and how Sam and Edith are. We congratulate Sam and Edith from our hearts and wish them all the best that's imaginable. Give our heartfelt regards to your benefactors. Your card, dear child, gave us indescribable joy, but it took 2 months to get here. May God give us peace. Sam should write us more often. Is he making any money? What are you doing?*

Heartfelt regards and kisses, Mutti.

Best regards to all, Betti.

Heartfelt regards, Papa.

Postcard from Mutti (in German)
Lwow, 18 October 1940

My most beloved boy, Guntherl,

Your sweet picture arrived a day after Yom Kippur. I don't have to mention, first of all, that we were very happy, and that we have been looking at it for a long time, as we often do. There is nothing today without melancholy. The drop of bitterness is that it has taken the picture 4 months to get here. It kills us [to think] *what you, dear boy, are doing today. We hear about the situation in London and can imagine very well what it's like. How is your health? Are you still with those people* [you are staying with]. *God protect all of you; may no one of you get affected* [by the war]. *Where about is Sam and Edith? Do you hear anything from him? We can't stand it any more thinking about Sam, Edith and you. As soon as possible, dear children. let us hear from you. Many good wishes for your benefactors. Betti is working in a beauty salon and earns her own money. Papa is a night watchman. May God give us soon a victorious peace. 1000 good wishes, greetings and kisses for you, Sam, Edith. From my heart* [in Yiddish] *Mama. Regards, Papa.*

To read in the papers what's going on in London one can go crazy. [in Yiddish, no doubt to pass the censor.]

Postcard from Mutti (in German)
Lwow, 18 February 1941

My dearest Guntherl!

We got 2 postcards from you today, from Nov. 4 and 18. May God bless you for your good, thankful heart. May you continue to be protected and saved from all dangers. May God continue to keep you in his grace that we may hear much good news from you. All of us thank you for your good wishes, may they be fulfilled. Dear child, my big boy. I answer every postcard of yours, does it get there? Who knows, perhaps we will soon not be able to write at all; then we will trust God and wait. Things were terrible in London, and who knows what may yet come. Why does Sam stay there? I beg you, dear boy, with all the strength of my love, tell me Sam's address, and write to him yourself. He should take pity on us and write us a postcard. I thank God that you are in good health and you should stay that way. We are in good health and hope to endure. I live with all of you in my thoughts. Everything in the crates has been sold. Even the crates have been used up. The suitcases are also almost empty. I now have my room and my kitchen looking pretty good. Uncle Munio and his family are doing relatively okay. I have lost thousands [of Polish currency] *because they were not exchanged in time. Betti is not employed because she lacks knowing the language. 1000 regards and kisses from Mutti. Please give our warm regards and many thanks to Family Corne.*

Dear Gunther, warmest regards, and continue to write often. Betti.

Regards, Papa.

Last Postcard from Mutti (in German) Lwow 14 March 1941

My Most Beloved Guntherl!

I'm sitting and writing to all my children who recently wrote to me. From you, child of my heart, I have the most mail. Our mail carrier is happy every time he comes to us, because he always gets something from us for his trouble. I would be very glad to hear from Sam as long as it is still possible to exchange letters. From 13 September till today times have been tough, and all I want to know is about [your/my?] health because there is no shortage of woes. Uncle Munio is happy to hear from you. He apologizes for not sending you a card because he lacks the patience for it. But he as well as Auntie send their best regards. Betti will never work here as a domestic because households in Poland are very run down. She was often at Shmuel Rosenblum's upscale shop and has gotten used to [like?] him. He has such a respectable character and fits well into the family. Perhaps Betti will soon find a job. May God grant us a peaceful summer; not like the previous one which we have not yet forgotten. We are in good health; only peace has to come like a miracle, unexpectedly. What is your weight? How tall are you now? What did you do with your white suit and the shoes? Many heartfelt regards to Family Corne. Simon wrote that he hopes to have you in America by J. [June/July?] '41. May it come true. Sam wrote that he would write more often, will it take ½ year again?

Letter from Sam to me
London, 26 August 1942

Old Boy,

I hoped to write you a few lines on my letter cards, but you must have taken an awful fancy to them. Anyway, they seem all to be gone, obliging me morally to write an ordinary-sized letter. Has its good sides, too, otherwise I might get completely out of practice. Well, that kind fellow at the door, attending to the switchboard very thoroughly fist and to you only after long reflection gave me the good news on the phone that the operation has been performed, and you are feeling well. He repeated this information today so that I feel I need not worry too much, after some unavoidable pain you will be quite o.k. again. (I know you would say H. P.) So, chin up in the meantime.

As to the outside world, I do not think you are missing much, except for a cheap ticket to Mrs. Miniver, which film we will have to see when you come out. Otherwise there is not much to attract you to "free London. We are provided with a daily "drop" of rain that keeps pouring down from the skies as if it was never going to stop and—for a change—we had an alert in daylight just as to remind us, there is still a war on. I hope you did not have to go to a shelter. We did not, although a keepsake of—as it seemed— decent size was dropped somewhere in our neighborhood (we heard the bang very distinctly) resulting in a warning given by our roof-spotter for our establishment. What a change, now that you are away these days! I feel quite lonely. We get so quickly used to fixed circumstances and habits, and we never realize this until a change occurs. I am staying at home all week in the evenings. You are not about, no lectures yet, no fire watch. I am becoming quite a bit of a hermit. But we shall make good for all of that in our holidays.

I suppose you are reading the daily papers. I thought the attached three periodicals might give you a break. The picture goer [movie review?] was unobtainable up to now. If I am lucky tomorrow I shall enclose it. Let me know, when you are coming back. Perhaps before Sunday so we could enjoy that day somewhere in the open air? I am fine and, touch wood (where is your head?), the pain has gone; this time, I hope, for good. I am anxious to see what you look like. Must be quite an Apollo now, and, no doubt, you will have to be double careful about those girls, who can't but go after any nice looking face. Well, see you soon. Keep smiling.

Yours, Sam

Made in the USA
San Bernardino, CA
10 October 2014